FY100

Fund Your $100,000

A Novel Initiative to Reduce Wealth Inequality

DANIEL J MEARS

DEDICATION

Bringing this big idea to reality will take effort. This book is in honor of those who will bring FY100 into existence.

FUND YOUR $100,000

CONTENTS

ACKNOWLEDGMENTS

Thank you, Mom and Dad, for laying the foundation for my understanding about the economy and the world.

1
FY100 – BIG IDEA

To effectively communicate the central premise of this book, I considered various ways to introduce the paradigm-shifting concepts it encompasses. One approach that came to mind was to begin with problem identification, in order to clearly illustrate the need for this novel way of thinking. Another option was to provide a history of systems, in order to give context and background information on how these concepts have evolved over time. A third possibility was to present a case study, which would demonstrate the interplay of these concepts in a relatable scenario.

After consideration, I have decided to present the main idea upfront, without any delays or teases. This approach allows the reader to fully understand and engage with the concept immediately, and to use this understanding to explore how it can impact themselves and society as a whole. The remainder of the book includes case examples, thoughts on implementation, how Fund Your Hundred relates to economic and political thought, impacts, and some thoughts on wealth inequality. I hope that you will find this journey engaging, informative, and ultimately worth enacting.

The Big Idea - Fund Your Hundred

Any person, company, organization, or government may give up to $100,000 to any American without having to pay any tax on those funds. The person receives the money in their Fund Your 100 account without any tax liability. Once $100,000 has been deposited by any combination of payers, no more funds may ever be deposited into the person's FY100 account.

The funds remain locked in the FY100 account until the account owner turns 65, at which time the funds become unlocked and may be withdrawn tax free and be used in any manner. The funds are not required to be withdrawn and may continue to grow tax free until the account holder chooses, or it is bequeathed to an heir into their FY100 account. An heir may receive any amount of bequeathed funds in excess of their own $100,000 contribution limit.

Any money deposited in FY100 accounts is invested in publicly traded domestic securities as determined to qualify by the Securities and Exchange Commission. The invested Class FY shares would be non-voting with dividends which are reinvested. All participants in the FY100 accounts will share equally in the dividend proceeds of the aggregate investment. No account holder earns more per share than any other account holder.

These three paragraphs largely cover this idea, which, when implemented, will begin to change the landscape of wealth inequality, retirement income, domestic public equity markets, and more. At this point, you may want to take time to contemplate what this policy framework would mean for you and those around you. Or, if you like, explore the other sections of this book to go into more depth of how this can be implemented, creating positive benefits on the American economy, and most importantly, on American lives.

2

FY100 - CASES

When an individual is aware that they will be receiving money into their Fund Your Hundred account, there are a variety of factors that they may consider, depending on their unique situation. These considerations can include things like their current financial situation, their future financial goals, or personal values and priorities when making decisions.

To better understand the types of factors that an individual may consider, let's consider a few specific scenarios created for this book.

Employed Family Man

In this first case, we will use Mr. Efm. He is married and has one adult child. For this scenario, let's assume the only FY100 contributions coming from someone else (to the giver's tax advantage) are coming from Mr. Efm's employer, a not-for-profit organization. This is a clear benefit for his employer, if these funds are coming in exchange for his regular compensation, Mr. Efm would need to agree to the amount applied because these funds would not be immediately available to him, as they would be locked, meaning unable to be accessed or spent, until he turned 65.

Let's say Mr. Efm agreed that his employer was to pay $10,000 of this year's compensation to his FY100 account, associated with his Social Security number. Mr. Efm's employer would not have to pay his portion of Medicare 1.45% or Social Security 6.2% taxes on that $10,000. That is $145 in Medicare and $620 in Social Security. Saving the employer $765 is a good deal for them. Perhaps they would be willing to share some of those savings with Mr. Efm, since he would not have access to those funds until he turns

65.

As an employee, Mr. Efm splits the total Medicare and Social Security tax owed with his employer, so he is also saving $765 that would have reduced his take home money on this $10,000 of compensation. Instead of $9,235, Mr. Efm will get the full $10,000, for the price of delaying when he can access the money when it unlocks when he turns 65.

That is not the end of his benefit though. Mr. Efm is a resident of Maryland, which has an income tax rate of 5.75%. Let's also apply a federal income tax owed of 22%. That is $575 in State income taxes and $2,200 in Federal income taxes. That $9,235 after Medicare and Social Security would have become $6,460 after income taxes were taken out. By putting the money into an FY100 account, Mr. Efm immediately has $3,540 more. He just has to wait 15 years to access it. In the meantime, that money will grow tax free.

Mr. Efm's spouse happens to be a year older than him. If he instead asks for the $10,000 to be applied to her FY100 account, associated with her Social Security number, his employer will get the same benefit on tax, and the Efm family would get the same benefit on tax. The difference would be, as a married couple, they could access those funds a year sooner, when she turns 65.

This is an interesting aspect of FY100 accounts. There is nothing that would prevent a person from having the funds for themself go to anyone else of their choosing, if the other person has not reached their own $100,000 FY100 account contribution limit. The funds can grow tax free in their account while locked until they turn age 65. Once unlocked at age 65, the funds can be withdrawn and used however the owner of the account wishes. Once withdrawn, the funds would be subject to all existing tax rules, like gifting limits, etc. So, your relationship with the other person and how they decide to use the funds are part of the equation.

For Mr. Efm's personal circumstance, he would not fund his, nor his wife's FY100 account first. Nor would he fund his son's. Instead, he would talk to his parents about funding each of their FY100 accounts first. Since both of his parents are over the age of 65, any funds going into the FY100 account associated with their Social Security numbers would go in unlocked. This means that the funds would be immediately accessible if they need them to be. Of course, if Mr. Efm directs the funds to his parents' accounts, it would be their money, which his parents ultimately would get to decide what to do with it.

In addition to the funds being unlocked since they are over 65, within the family they have more accounts with which to direct tax advantaged money. If it were just Mr. Efm, and he could direct $10,000 per year, he would exhaust his own $100,000 FY100 account contribution limit in 10 years. By using both his parents, his wife, and himself, they would combined have $400,000 FY100 account contribution limit in their family. That would take 40 years to fill, with just Mr. Efm's annual $10,000 FY100 contribution.

Senior Couple

Mr. Efm's parents have their own scenarios to consider. His father, Om Efm, is retired and has income from an employer pension as well as Social Security income. His mother, Ol Efm, had also worked and was able to save money in a 401(k). She is taking required distributions from the 401(k) as well as receiving her Social Security Income. Both are retired and do not have an employer to provide them with new compensation. This does not prevent them from benefiting from contributing to their own FY100 accounts.

Om Efm's income from both his pension and his Social Security are subject to ordinary income tax. By contributing his pension income and his Social Security to the FY100 account, associated with his Social Security number, he would not have to pay ordinary incomes taxes on that money up to his $100,000 contribution limit. With his level of income, he will reach the contribution limit in just over two years. Since Om Efm is over 65, all those contributions to his FY100 are unlocked and available to use right away in any manner he wishes.

Ol Efm is in the same situation as her husband. Everything she would contribute to the FY100 from her 401(k) disbursements and her Social Security Income would not be subject to ordinary income tax. In her case, if she contributes all these income sources, she will reach her $100,000 contribution in almost four years. If they would like to accelerate their contributions, Om Efm could begin contributing to his wife's FY100 once his is maximized in less than three years. This would enable them both to maximize their accounts a few months sooner.

The senior Efm's are not expected to reach their FY100 contribution limit quickly. Since the FY100 funds will grow tax free, the couple will not want to withdraw those funds to pay their living expenses.

The senior Efm's have been using their retirement income and Social Security income to pay for their living expenses in retirement. In addition to food, utilities, household, and other expenses, the senior Efm's have four years of payments left on their mortgage, they give generously to their church, and save some money for some small trips in retirement. They also have over $90,000 in investments outside of their retirement accounts which has continued to slowly grow since they retired.

Since they are living off their income, the idea of putting all their income into the FY100 accounts right now does not make the most sense to them. If they do put their income in the accounts, they will save on the income tax they would otherwise have to pay. However, they would also need to withdraw quite a bit from the FY100 accounts right away for their living expenses. This would inhibit them from taking advantage of the other very beneficial side of FY100 accounts. The investment growth and withdrawals from the FY100 accounts are tax free as well.

The senior Efm's recognize they still have a few years of a small mortgage deduction from the interest on their home loan, which they would still like to get while paying off the loan. In addition, their outside investments of over $90,000 will be growing with the need to pay capital gains taxes on future growth. If the same investment were in their FY100 accounts, any future growth would be tax free.

They decide to quickly direct $90,000 of their income to their FY100 accounts, $45,000 in each, and use the $90,000 in outside investments for their living expenses until it is exhausted. They will not put all of their income toward the FY100 accounts, as they will keep a little bit out to take advantage of the mortgage deduction.

After paying off their mortgage, the senior Efm's decide to direct a little more than those payments toward the $110,000 remaining in their combined contribution limits in their FY100 accounts. With $17,000 per year freed up from their mortgage expense, they will fully fund their FY100 accounts in less than six years after the mortgage is paid off. Their plan is for those accounts to grow, until they are bequeathed to their heirs, their two children, as unlocked funds which are allocated to each child's FY100 account. Those funds will be part of the senior Efm's estate, and will continue to grow tax free, until they are withdrawn from those FY100 accounts.

Single Underemployed Woman

Ms. Suw is a single mother with one young child. Her circumstances are among the most challenging, in that she is only able to work infrequently, as she has no dependable or affordable childcare. Additionally, she has no other family able to assist her financially and often has trouble meeting her basic needs, and she relies on public assistance for housing, food, and medical expenses. When Ms. Suw does work, all of her income goes to her expenses, and she has nothing remaining to be able to save for retirement, let alone other goals.

When Ms. Suw does work, the jobs do not offer pension benefits, nor do they offer access to 401(k), 403(b), or 457 accounts. Furthermore, even if they did, she would not be able to make any employee contributions to them, as she needs all of her income for her living expenses. The same holds for an IRA or Roth IRA account. Since she works so little, she is not earning much towards the Social Security formula. This means when she is old enough to qualify for Social Security, these benefits will be on the low end.

The main options for retirement savings do not work for Ms. Suw. Increases to contribution limits do not benefit her, opt out enrollment in a 401(k) does not work, as she would immediately opt out, because she needs money to live today. Even if she did set aside some funds to go into an IRA, the money would either be taxed going in (Roth) or when the proceeds came out (Traditional).

The FY100 is structured a bit differently than other options. Combining a great benefit from Traditional IRAs, not taxing the qualifying contributions, with a great benefit of Roth IRAs, not taxing the qualifying withdrawals, Ms. Suw would be better off depositing her money into an FY100 than either IRA type.

In all likelihood, with Ms. Suw's circumstances, she will not be putting any money into an FY100 herself. She would need someone else to give for her, and this is where the FY100 has a greater promise over the other options.

Since the person putting money into an FY100 does not need to pay tax on the contribution, even if it is to someone else's account, there is a greater chance of a benefactor helping out Ms. Suw. In this case she was speaking with an older couple, Ol and Om Efm at her church. There is a new program of the church where collections were being taken up to help people fund their FY100 accounts. The senior Efm's have been strong supporters of their church community and they are going to give some toward the church's FY100 effort. They even state they will donate some more once their mortgage has been paid.

Both Ms. Suw and her young daughter qualify for the church's program, and contributions from the church members will slowly accumulate in each of their FY100 accounts. This money will certainly help her in her senior years, and since contributions are being made so early for her daughter, they will have a very long time to grow, and be of even greater benefit for her when she turns 65, several decades from now.

Wealthy Young Lady

A very different scenario is for Ms. Wyl. She is not married and does not have any children. She works at a very good job in a high-priced city. In addition to getting a high salary, she is eligible for an annual bonus from her company, which the prior year was $200,000 for her.

As a for profit corporation, Ms. Wyl's employer has an additional incentive for its employees to accept compensation in an FY100 account. In addition to not having to pay the employer portion on payroll taxes of Medicare and Social Security, up to 7.65% of qualifying payroll, the employer can also save on their corporate income taxes. In this case that is an additional 21%.

In the best case for the employer, an employee would accept the full $100,000 of compensation, allowing the employer to avoid paying 28.65% in taxes on the $100,000. Since the company can save up to $28,650 in taxes when an employee accepts $100,000 in compensation, they offer an additional incentive of $15,000 for every $100,000 an employee participates.

This is a strong incentive for Ms. Wyl. With her $200,000 bonus, the company would instead give her $230,000 in annual bonus. With her high salary, this income has an income tax rate of 35%, or $80,500. Since her annual salary exceeded the Social Security wage limit, which is the maximum amount on which Social Security taxes are paid, she does not have the 6.2% tax to pay on that extra compensation. She would owe the 1.45% Medicare tax, or $3,335. By contributing all of that to FY100 accounts, she will save $83,835 in income and payroll taxes.

Ms. Wyl annually contributes the maximum amount to her 401(k) and her Traditional IRA. By adding a $100,000 contribution to her FY100 account she will maximize her retirement savings. Since the FY100 limits lifetime contributions in an individual's account to $100,000, Ms. Wyl will have $130,000 that she cannot save for herself. She decides to give $65,000 to each of her parents FY100 accounts, associated with their Social Security numbers.

The following year, Ms. Wyl's employer gives her a $200,000 bonus again. Since the financial benefit to the employer remains for the compensation going into FY100 accounts, they offer the same incentive as the year before, meaning $230,000 is available again. Since Ms. Wyl would again be faced with $83,835 in payroll and income taxes, she would prefer the money go to others. Her parents had not made any of their own FY100 contributions in the past year, so she finishes funding each of their accounts with $35,000 each. That is $70,000, leaving her with $160,000.

Ms. Wyl's only sister is married and they have one young child. After speaking with them, she directs $54,000 to each of the FY100 accounts associated with their three Social Security numbers. She used $2,000 of her regular income to round up, this saved her over $700 in income and payroll taxes.

In the third year, she is again offered the bonus and incentive of $230,000. Ms. Wyl's sister had contributed $8,000 into her daughter's FY100 over the past year, so Ms. Wyl gave them the remaining $130,000 to fully fund their lifetime cap in each of their three FY100 accounts. This leaves her with $100,000 that she could contribute to FY100 accounts. She talks to her grandparents, aunts, uncles, and cousins. She splits the remaining $100,000 among all of them.

In the fourth year, the employer and her tax incentives remain, so again she has $230,000 to contribute to FY100 accounts. In the previous year, she got married, so she fully funds her spouse's lifetime FY100 account associated with their Social Security number. She again evenly distributes the remaining funds among her grandparents, aunts, uncles, and cousins.

When she has her first child the following year, she can fully fund her daughter's FY100 account associated with her Social Security number. She knows that this money will grow tax free for the next 65 years and be able to provide her daughter with great financial security in her senior years. This year, and in the years to come she is incentivized to continue to share her the good fortune of her high income with her family, close friends, and explore opportunities for giving to those in her community that would have a need for a benefactor like her.

Ultra-High Net Worth Individual

Mr. Uhnwi has already signed up for the Giving Pledge. Having amassed a significant amount of wealth through the rapid growth of his business, Mr. Uhnwi was compensated largely in restricted stock which grew over time. Now in his early sixties, he is no longer the CEO of his company, but does have a Board seat. He also spends his time with a few charities he has funded by selling some of his restricted stock. Additionally, he also diversifies his investments when he is able to sell his restricted stock by buying other stock in both public and private equity markets, as well as land, treasuries, and commodities.

Since he has been so successful, Mr. Uhnwi has no unmet needs for himself or anyone in his family, and his participation in the Giving Pledge enables him to know that he will be able to benefit many others from his success.

Upon discovering the ability to use the FY100 provisions to provide benefit to himself and others, he saw promise in its use. $100,000 is an insignificant amount of money for Mr. Uhnwi. With a very large annual tax burden he is always looking for legal opportunities to avoid paying tax, and maximize his investment return as well as the good he can do funding charities. Right away, he fully funds the FY100 accounts of family and many close friends, since the tax advantage is very attractive.

As a member of the board for his company, he takes the lead in offering incentives and bonuses for his employees to fund the FY100 accounts of his employees, their families, and those they choose to give to. He makes these incentive policies permanent, so they will benefit all new employees and encourage all his employees to reach further out in their communities to spread the giving once they have reached their FY100 lifetime caps.

His company has historically had corporate giving as part of its mission. In order to further benefit the locations where they had corporate locations, Mr. Uhnwi helped craft a new corporate giving program. It would contribute directly to people in those communities, who otherwise would not be able to fund their own FY100 accounts. The people who work in the communities where his business is located provide services and help support his business and his employees, so their stability and success is very important to him. As a further step, Mr. Uhnwi crafted a program where customers could benefit from customer incentives, rebates, and other promotions that returned funds back to his loyal customer base in FY100 contributions. Mr. Uhnwi sees the benefits of these policies for his employees and his customers, in addition to the business itself.

The charities that Mr. Uhnwi is involved in give out millions of dollars each year for food assistance, health, and education. All of these are worthwhile and get at some of the symptoms of the challenges in society that create inequality, disparate access, and uneven opportunity. He sees the benefits of redistribution of wealth across society, enabling people to care for themselves adequately, particularly in their later years, when they no longer have employment income. In some cases, they will even be able to share wealth with their heirs, which might not have been possible otherwise. This will assist their young relatives in later meeting their goals.

With the lifetime cap on contributing to FY100 accounts, Mr. Uhnwi can see that while the incentives for contributing to these accounts are stronger than any other investment vehicle, they have little appeal to the wealthy. The strong tax incentives combined with the ease of contributing directly to others encourages assets to be spread across society. The only way for a business or individual to continue to capitalize on the tax advantages is that they must continue to spread money further and further out. Recipients are also strongly encouraged to accept these funds with stronger tax incentives than any other retirement savings vehicle. The ability for the recipient to grow the balance tax free encourages saving, and if possible, passing the assets to their heirs with a continuation of the tax benefits beyond their lifetime.

3
FY100 - IMPLEMENTATION

Tax Code

The United States tax code is the system designed to collect revenue from individuals and businesses to fund the government's operations and programs. It is contained in the Internal Revenue Code (IRC), which is a set of federal laws that outline how taxes are to be calculated, collected, and enforced.

The provisions of the tax code can be broadly grouped into three categories:

- Tax rates: The tax code specifies different tax rates for distinct types of income and for different tax brackets. For example, there are different tax rates for wages and salaries, investment income, and business income. The tax code also specifies different tax rates for different tax brackets, which are based on an individual's taxable income.

- Deductions and credits: The tax code allows taxpayers to claim deductions and credits to reduce their taxable income and thus their tax liability. Deductions are amounts that can be subtracted from a taxpayer's taxable income to lower the amount of income that is subject to tax. Credits are amounts that can be subtracted directly from a taxpayer's tax liability.

- Compliance and enforcement: The tax code outlines the rules and procedures that individuals and businesses must follow when filing their tax returns and paying their taxes. It also outlines the penalties for noncompliance and the procedures for appealing a tax decision.

The implementation of the policy recommendations of the Fund Your Hundred initiative will need to take place within the Tax Code. However, I will not be suggesting specific sections or language for the FY100 initiative to be added to this book. There are many skilled professionals, such as policy analysts, tax experts, and legal professionals, who are familiar with the Tax Code and can effectively incorporate the FY100 initiative's elements as policy. They can also ensure that there are no unintended consequences or conflicts that arise as a result of the initiative's implementation.

The Internal Revenue Code will need to address three main areas in relation to the FY100 initiative. The first area is the tracking and taxation of contributions made by third parties to another person's FY100 account. The code will need to specify how these contributions will be traced back to the taxpayer and which taxes they will be exempt from with each contribution. If a third party makes a contribution to an unrelated person's FY100 account, the code will need to address the income taxes that can be claimed as a deduction as a result of that contribution for the contributor. Additionally, for contributions made to employees, the code will need to outline the employment taxes that can also be claimed as a deduction if the contributions are being made in place of regular compensation.

The second area of consideration for FY100 contributions is the tax implications for the recipient. It is the responsibility of the recipient to account for any income or employment taxes that would have been owed on the value of the contribution. These deductions apply regardless of where the funds are coming from, whether it is from an employer as compensation, a third-party source, or if the account holder is funding it solely from their own resources. It is important to note that receiving funding from others, particularly from employers, may present the greatest opportunity to offset tax liability.

The next important aspect for the code to address is the withdrawal of assets by the FY100 account holder. Specifically, the code must ensure that proceeds from an FY100 account are not subject to taxation. This applies to both the account holder's own assets and any inherited assets. The code should ensure that withdrawals of these assets do not trigger capital gains taxes, income taxes, or any other form of tax liability. This is a crucial aspect of the code as it ensures that the account holder can access and use their assets without being penalized by taxes, thus promoting the intended purpose of the FY100 account.

Searchable Database

The foundation of the FY100 initiative will be built on a searchable database that caters to the needs of its users. To make it easy for both givers and receivers to use, the database should have a simple and user-friendly interface. Additionally, the FY100 database should include several key features to ensure that transactions are properly recorded and tracked. This includes accurate records of contributions and their recipients, permissions to control who can view certain information, the ability to designate beneficiaries, a record of all contributions, and potentially demographic data to help givers make informed decisions. With these features in place, the FY100 database will be able to support the initiative's goal of facilitating contributions to the account holders.

In order for the FY100 initiative to be widely adopted and accessible to the greatest number of users, it must be made available on a variety of platforms. This will make it easy for users to access the program and transfer funds quickly and seamlessly and monitor the FY100 account.

Additionally, it is important to implement robust security measures to protect user information and prevent fraud. This includes ensuring that personal and financial information is kept private and secure, and that the account holder is in full control of their account. This will help to build trust and confidence in the system, making it more likely that users will adopt and utilize the FY100 initiative. In addition, it will be important to implement measures to detect and prevent unauthorized access to accounts, and to provide a mechanism for users to report any suspicious activity or fraud. Overall, security and privacy are essential elements for the successful adoption and use of the FY100 initiative.

■ Giver

The person or entity providing the funds needs a straightforward system for transferring money to a recipient's FY100 account. For this system to be effective, it must include an account that links the giver with their desired tax identification number. This is important because it allows the giver to specify how they want to be identified for tax purposes. For example, a small business owner may want to have an account that is associated with their business, using the business's tax identification number. Alternatively, they may want to give funds as an individual, using their own Social Security number. This flexibility in identifying oneself for tax purposes is important for the giver as it enables them to make contributions in a way that aligns with their personal or business tax strategy.

In either case, whether the giver is contributing funds as an individual or as a business, the system for transferring funds to the recipient's FY100 account must generate a tax record. This record should include the following information: the amount of the contribution, the recipient of the funds, and the date of the funding. By linking this record with the giver's tax identification, it will enable them to apply the tax benefits associated with the contribution in an appropriate and accurate way. This tax record will serve as proof of the contribution for tax purposes and provide the giver with the necessary documentation to claim any applicable tax benefits. This is important for both the giver and the recipient, as it ensures that the contribution is properly accounted for and that any potential tax benefits are maximized.

To ensure that the funds are transferred to the correct person, the database that manages the FY100 accounts should include the ability to search for individuals by their Social Security number (SSN). This will enable the giver to easily locate the recipient's account and transfer the funds accordingly. To use this feature, the giver will need to obtain the recipient's SSN, which they can ask the recipient for directly. This feature is essential for ensuring that the funds are delivered to the intended person, and that the giver is able to verify the recipient's identity. Additionally, using the SSN for identifying the recipient also ensures that the information is kept private and secure.

There may be scenarios where a giver wishes to make contributions to unknown parties. To accommodate this, the database that manages the FY100 accounts should be designed to be broadly searchable using various demographic data. For example, a giver may want to contribute to infants who were born in the previous year and live in their county. The database should allow the giver to search for individuals based on their date of birth and county of residence. This would provide a general list of people who are willing to accept funds. It's important to note that the returned list should not include individually identifying information to protect the recipient's privacy. If the recipient is willing to receive funds, that can be designated in their FY100 account, and the giver can make the contribution. This feature allows givers to make contributions to specific groups of individuals, such as infants in their county, while still maintaining the privacy of the recipients.

- ### Receiver

To be eligible to receive funds for an FY100 account, individuals must have a valid Social Security number. However, to activate the account and make it ready to receive funds, there are a few additional requirements that the individual must meet. These include:

- Verifying their contact information: The individual must provide accurate contact information, such as their address, phone number, and email address, so that the account can be properly linked to them.

- Associating their date of birth with the account: The individual must provide their date of birth to confirm their identity and ensure that the funds are properly unlocked when they meet the requirements.

- Designating a beneficiary: The individual must designate a beneficiary, who will be the person or entity that will receive the funds in the event that the account holder passes away.

Once these requirements have been met, the individual is considered to be eligible to receive funds for their FY100 account. This process is designed to ensure that only eligible individuals are able to receive funds and that the funds are directed to the intended recipient.

When making FY100 accounts available to everyone with a Social Security number, certain challenges may arise for some individuals. These challenges can include issues such as insecure housing, health conditions that make it difficult to access the account, or a lack of ability to access the account independently. To address these challenges, the system must include provisions for third-party guardians or administrators to act on behalf of those who are unable to manage their own accounts.

For example, minors, incapacitated individuals, and others receiving care may require a parent or guardian to act on their behalf in managing their FY100 account. In these cases, existing systems for third-party management of accounts can be utilized, rather than creating a new process. This will ensure that all individuals, regardless of their ability to manage their own accounts, are able to access the benefits of an FY100 account.

Additionally, the database must be able to accommodate individuals with insecure housing. This means that, at a minimum, the database should have a reliable way to communicate with the account owner, such as a phone number, email address, or other contact information. This will enable account recovery and other forms of communication as needed.

The establishment of a beneficiary is a crucial step in the process of managing funds in an FY100 account. A beneficiary is a person or entity that is designated to receive the funds from the account in case of the account holder's death. There are only two ways for the funds to be removed from the account. The first way is for the account holder to withdraw the funds for any reason, once the funds in it are unlocked, when the individual reaches the age of 65. The second way is at the time of death of the FY100 account holder. The funds in the account, whether they are locked or unlocked, will be transferred to the beneficiary or any contingent beneficiaries' FY100 accounts. This ensures that the funds in the FY100 account are protected and will be used for the intended purpose.

Additionally, the date of birth of the account holder is another important criteria that must be associated with the FY100 account. While the Social Security number of the account holder should already have a date of birth associated with it, this additional step ensures that the funds in the account are unlocked at the appropriate time. When funds are deposited in an account, they are locked and cannot be withdrawn until the FY100 account holder reaches the age of 65. The date that the funds will be unlocked is calculated based on the FY100 account holder's date of birth. Any interest dividends earned on the deposited funds will also be unlocked on the same date.

When an account holder reaches the age of 65, the funds they have deposited into their FY100 account, along with any interest dividends that have accumulated, will become unlocked and accessible for withdrawal. This is an important feature of the system, as it ensures that FY100 account holders will have access to their funds at the appropriate time.

It is important to note that if an account holder passes away before reaching the age of 65, the funds in their FY100 account will be transferred to their designated beneficiary or beneficiaries. However, these inherited funds will remain locked until the bequeathing party would have reached the age of 65.

The system must be able to track and distinguish between locked and unlocked funds within an account. For example, let's say a 35-year-old account holder has deposited $14,000 into their FY100 account. These funds and any interest dividends that have accumulated will be locked until the account holder reaches the age of 65. If the account holder is a beneficiary of someone older than 65 who passed away and inherits $70,000, these funds will be deposited into the FY100 account as unlocked money. The database must be able to track and separate the locked funds of $14,000, including the accrued interest dividends on those locked funds, from the unlocked funds of $70,000, including the accrued interest dividends on those funds. This will ensure that account holders have access to their funds at the appropriate time and that the system is able to accurately track and manage FY100 account balances.

When an account holder is eligible to receive funds, they may choose to include additional information about themselves that is searchable. This information should be under the control of the account holder and could include things like high school graduation information. For example, if an account holder includes the high school they graduated from, along with their graduation year, they may be able to receive funds from benefactors who wish to make contributions to their classmates from their graduating year. In this case, the benefactor may not know the individual identities of the list of people from their search, but they will need to know how much they can contribute. In this case, the benefactor would need to see that $14,000 had been contributed towards the $100,000 lifetime contribution limit on the account. They would then know that they could contribute up to $86,000 more.

The system must be able to track the total amount of contributions made to an account, including the contribution date, in order to calculate the appropriate dividends based on the dividend distribution schedule and ensure that the full lifetime contribution limit is available. For example, if an account has a balance of $21,000, it may be that $19,000 was contributed and $2,000 of the balance was dividends. This would enable the system to know that $81,000 more could be contributed before reaching the lifetime contribution limit.

Federal Government

The establishment of FY100 accounts aims to reduce federal government involvement in retirement savings and wealth building, but there is still a crucial role for government in the initiative. The federal government will act as the central hub for all FY100 account data and will need to collaborate with the SEC, IRS, and SSA to ensure the smooth operation of the initiative. The Social Security Administration will be responsible for the establishment and maintenance of each account, and the government will need to work closely with the Internal Revenue Service to apply tax advantages for both contributors and recipients. Additionally, coordination with the Securities and Exchange Commission to oversee the administration of publicly traded equities and dividend distributions. This coordinated effort between government and the SEC, IRS, and SSA is essential to ensure the success of the FY100 initiative.

■ Social Security Administration

Since every person with a Social Security number will be eligible for an FY100 account the federal government plays a crucial role in the establishment and maintenance of the FY100 accounts. The coordination of the Social Security Administration (SSA) is essential for ensuring that every person with a Social Security number can establish and maintain an account. The SSA will need to be ready to receive new customers, including those who may not currently have a Social Security number, such as minor children, individuals who belong to groups that object to government programs, or others. People needing to resolve issues with their Social Security number may be more motivated to do so, when also wanting to begin depositing funds into an FY100 account. This coordination will also help to resolve any issues related to a person's Social Security number.

To ensure the integrity and reliable operation of these accounts, there will need to be close coordination between the databases of the SSA and another federal agency if they administer the FY100 accounts. Changes in status, address and other information will need to be regularly cross-checked. While it may be an option for the FY100 account data to be incorporated into the Social Security database, since the FY100 account will be functioning more like an investment or banking account, with regular external access, the security of the database would likely benefit from a gap between two databases, or sufficient firewalls.

■ Securities and Exchange Commission

The Social Security Administration would be responsible for overseeing the FY100 accounts, while the Securities and Exchange Commission (SEC) would oversee the investments made under the FY100 initiative. This is because the SEC is a federal agency that already has regulatory and oversight responsibilities for the public equity markets. In other words, the task of overseeing investments made under the initiative would be a logical extension of the SEC's existing duties.

The FY100 initiative is expected to generate a significant amount of funds which will be deposited into collective accounts. These funds are expected to reach trillions of dollars. A large portion of these funds will be locked and will not be available for withdrawal for a significant period of time, some of which could be decades. This presents a unique investment mix that will require a different approach to management compared to traditional equity accounts, retirement accounts, bank accounts, treasuries, and other federal funds. The funds being locked for a long period of time, and the scale of the funds involved, will require specialized management techniques that differ from those typically used for managing other types of investment accounts.

Assuming a relatively even distribution of deposits across age groups, the initiative's investment strategy will have a very long time horizon, since the funds cannot be withdrawn until the FY100 account holder reaches age 65. This means that nearly half of the deposits will be locked for over three decades. This long-time horizon will allow the investment strategy to focus heavily on the long-term, which can provide significant stability to the investments that receive the funds.

Because of the long-term nature of these investments, the SEC will have the flexibility to offer funds to securities that provide a strong dividend return, rather than focusing on short-term fluctuations in stock values. The SEC will make funds available for investments that have and hold a class of share value of $1 and remain at $1. The return will come from dividends, which will be reinvested back into the account holders' accounts as additional FY shares of $1 each. This approach will help to minimize the impact of short-term fluctuations in stock values and instead focus on long-term, stable investments that will provide a steady income stream for the account holders over the long term.

The SEC, as part of its mandate to protect investors, maintain fair, orderly and efficient markets, and facilitate capital formation, already collects data on publicly traded companies. This information can be used to identify the fundamentals of the domestic publicly traded equities that could participate in the FY100 investments.

To select suitable investment parameters for the initiative, the SEC will carefully evaluate the fundamentals of potential companies. This will include assessing their time horizons, dividend potential, and capacity to absorb capital and meet return goals. Using this data, the SEC will identify companies that meet these criteria and are well-positioned for the initiative. These eligible companies will then be able to seek FY100 funds.

The SEC, as the agency responsible for overseeing the investments made under the initiative, should have a system in place to deal with organizations that are unable to meet their dividend projections. This system should include measures to protect the interests of the account holders and the integrity of the initiative.

One approach could involve scaling back on the invested capital in organizations that are struggling to meet their projections. This would help to minimize the potential of dividend losses for the account holders and ensure that their funds are not tied up in underperforming investments.

Another approach could involve lowering the time horizon for guaranteed funding for organizations that are unable to meet their projections. This would limit the amount of time that account holders' funds would be tied up in underperforming investments, while still allowing the organization an opportunity to improve its performance.

Finally, the SEC could also consider restricting organizations that are unable to meet their projections from accessing FY100 account investments altogether. This would help to safeguard the interests of the account holders and ensure that their funds are not invested in organizations that are unlikely to provide the desired returns.

As the agency responsible for overseeing the investments made under the initiative, the SEC should offer a variety of investment options that are tailored to the different needs and preferences of businesses. Some businesses may prefer longer time horizons, while others may prefer shorter time horizons. Similarly, some businesses may want to take on a large amount of capital, while others may want to take on a smaller amount.

It is the task of the SEC to structure the investment offerings in a way that will benefit account holders through dividend returns. This can be achieved by offering investment packages with different investment criteria, based on the time horizon, amount of capital, and other factors that are important to businesses.

Since the investment returns will be averaged and then distributed among all account holders, it is reasonable for there to be varying dividend returns based upon the investment criteria set up by the SEC for different investment packages. This allows for the FY100 initiative to have a more diversified investment portfolio and to have the opportunity to earn higher returns.

- **Federal Reserve**

The introduction of FY100 accounts, which will be managed by the Social Security Administration and dividend investments overseen by the Securities and Exchange Commission, will provide a new and powerful tool for the Federal Reserve to use in its role of managing United States monetary policy. The Federal Reserve is responsible for implementing policies that help maintain price stability and full employment in the economy.

To achieve these goals, the Federal Reserve has a range of tools at its disposal, including:

- The Federal Funds Rate, which is the interest rate at which depository institutions lend and borrow money overnight.

- The Discount Rate, which is the interest rate at which depository institutions borrow money from the Federal Reserve.

- The Reserve Requirement, which is the amount of money that depository institutions must hold in reserve against their deposits.

The introduction of these new accounts will provide the Federal Reserve with another tool to manage monetary policy. The Federal Reserve can use these accounts as a way to influence the economy. This will enable the Federal Reserve to more effectively implement monetary policy and to achieve its goals of price stability and full employment.

With the introduction of FY100 accounts, the Federal Reserve will have two new means of affecting its monetary policies. The first is to directly invest in FY100 accounts, which would serve to directly increase the available money supply. The funds that are added into individual's accounts would then be available directly for investment into publicly traded domestic institutions established by the SEC. This would be an alternative to providing stimulus checks directly to taxpayers or other federal stimulus programs. It would be broad-based and able to direct funds to large portions of the United States population, without being directly available to most account holders for immediate consumption needs. This method would not carry the same inflationary risk as direct stimulus payments.

The other opportunity available to the Federal Reserve would be on the investment side of the account. Instead of offering traditional Treasury bonds and other Treasury securities, the Federal Reserve would be able to invest in some of the packages offered by the SEC. This could be utilized to serve as a backstop in cases of insufficient demand for capital, or it could be utilized to remove capital opportunities from the publicly traded domestic securities and reducing the overall supply of the capital. The Federal Reserve could initiate the acquisition of Treasury securities from available FY100 funds. This would give the Federal Reserve more flexibility in managing monetary policy and achieving its goals.

Investing directly in FY100 accounts is a powerful tool and is very positive for the FY100 account holders, however, once the Federal Reserve has invested in these accounts, it will not be able to undo the investment, so it would need to be undertaken with certainty.

By working with the SEC on the investment side, the Federal Reserve would be able to invest in some of the packages offered by the SEC. This would give the Federal Reserve more flexibility to change strategies and adjust the takedown and interest levels on the invested funds. By working with shorter-term investment packages, the Federal Reserve may participate in packages with high interest or secure funds over longer time horizons, depending on the needs of the broader economy. This would provide the Federal Reserve with a more versatile approach to manage the money supply and stabilize the economy.

▪ The Legislature

The establishment of the FY100 initiative as law would provide the Senate and the House of Representatives with a new tool for advancing their policy objectives. Instead of relying solely on traditional methods such as stimulus payments, tax rebates, or tax incentives, Congress would have the option to utilize the FY100 accounts as a means of distributing resources to their constituents.

One advantage of using the FY100 accounts for policy implementation is the ability to target specific regions, disaster-impacted areas, or population groups. Additionally, the accounts offer a more efficient way of reaching people compared to traditional methods such as tax rebates or stimulus payments, which are typically only available to taxpayers or individuals with established connections to banks through the Internal Revenue Service.

Furthermore, similar to the Federal Reserve, Congress may want to use the accounts to distribute resources into the economy with a lower likelihood of inflationary impacts. The FY100 accounts provide an alternative way of injecting funds into the economy, which can help mitigate inflationary pressures caused by more traditional forms of stimulus. Overall, the FY100 accounts offer Congress a versatile and efficient tool for advancing their policy objectives and providing support to their constituents.

The use of stimulus payments as a means of providing financial support to individuals has been a common practice in recent years. However, there are certain limitations to this method of distribution. For example, individuals who have established a direct deposit link with the Internal Revenue Service (IRS) will typically receive their payments automatically, while others may need to wait for a physical check to be mailed to their address. Additionally, stimulus payments are typically only distributed to individuals who file tax returns, which means that certain individuals, such as dependents, minors, or individuals who do not file tax returns, may not be able to receive these payments.

On the other hand, the proposed accounts would provide a novel way to distribute funds to a wider range of individuals. For example, contributions to the accounts can reach dependents, minors, and others who do not have an active tax return. Furthermore, unlike stimulus payments, the contributions to the accounts would be locked for those under the age of 65, which would mean that these funds would be available later for many FY100 account holders. However, this also means that account holders who have already met their lifetime contribution cap would not be eligible to receive these federal transfers, unless there is specific authorizing legislation to increase the cap or waive it for that particular stimulus.

Over time, as more people reach their lifetime contribution cap, the remaining people with available space for FY100 account contributions will structurally further away from capital available to be transferred. Congress may see a time when completing the transfers of capital to maximize everyone's lifetime cap may make good policy sense. With complete funding, FY100 accounts may serve as a mechanism to reduce reliance on the Social Security system.

There are under four million babies born in the US each year. If each were to be funded with $100,000 in their FY100 account at birth, that would have an annual expense of under $400 billion each year. With Social Security expenditures at over $1.2 trillion a transition to a front-loaded retirement funding scenario could cost less than a third of paying for retirement benefits through employment taxes. After 65 years, a $100,000 contribution would grow to over $4.4 million with 6% compounded interest.

State Government

The role that State government could play in the proposed initiative would likely involve the state pension systems, state unemployment, or other benefit programs offered by the State. Like the federal government,

States have a significant role in the social and economic welfare of its citizens.

One potential way that State government could utilize the initiative is by incorporating it into their unemployment insurance system. State unemployment systems use taxes or fees to finance the initiative, and the funds are managed by the state government to provide benefits to eligible individuals who have lost their jobs. Currently, only a portion of unemployment benefits are taxed by Social Security. While this means there is less depletion of their current income benefit, it also has an effect on their Social Security benefit calculation. Unemployment benefits are not typically included in a person's Social Security benefit calculation, as Social Security does not count unemployment benefits as earned income. An option for State government would be to include an FY100 contribution to benefit their resident at a time when they are not adding to their Social Security calculation.

Another potential use for the initiative could be in State pension systems. Depending on the state, these pension systems may be underfunded. The retirement security of State workers, as well as local government and school district employees who may utilize the State pension system, is important. By contributing to FY100 accounts of their pension members, States may find that it provides a valuable option to provide a tax-advantaged defined contribution benefit to these employees. This could help to provide additional retirement security for State employees.

4

FY100 - CREATIVE DISTRIBUTION

One of the main obstacles in current systems for funding retirement is the limitations on how the money can be earned. IRAs, 401(k)s, 403(b)s, and 457s are all savings plans that allow individuals to accumulate assets that can be used to generate income during retirement, or to draw down on over time to cover living expenses. However, to participate in these plans, individuals must have earned income. While IRAs can be used by anyone with earned income, the other plans require an employer-sponsored plan to participate. Unfortunately, about half of American households do not have access to these employer-sponsored plans, which limits their ability to save for retirement through these means.

To determine your Social Security benefit and maximize its value, you must calculate your benefit using your highest 35 earning years. The benefit is closely tied to employment history, or being married to an employed person, which means that it is primarily an income program, rather than a mechanism to build wealth. Unlike other retirement programs, it does not provide a way to accumulate assets that can be passed along to others.

The main difference between Social Security and other retirement programs is that Social Security is an income program, which means that it is designed to provide a steady stream of income to retirees to help cover living expenses. It is not intended to be a way to build wealth or pass along assets to future generations. However, it does offer survivor benefits, which can provide some additional financial support to surviving family members.

It is also important to note that Social Security is a government-funded program, which is funded through payroll taxes and its benefits are determined by the taxes paid and the number of years the individual has worked. Social Security is an important source of retirement income for many people, but it is not intended to provide enough income to cover all of a retiree's expenses and it is not a replacement for other savings and investment plans.

Fund Your Hundred accounts are intended to build wealth, particularly for the half of Americans who currently lack any meaningful assets. The concept of wealth inequality is often described in various ways, such as how a small number of people possess as much wealth as half of all Americans, or how 60% of American households have less wealth than the top 1%. The specific numbers may vary depending on the data source used and the definition of assets, but the overall message is consistent: a significant portion of wealth is concentrated in the hands of a small number of individuals, leaving many without any assets or even in debt. This highlights the need for an initiative that can help increase the wealth of those who currently lack it.

The goal of FY100 initiative is to aggressively pursue getting every person in America with a Social Security number, $100,000 in wealth, which would be preserved until they turn 65. When looked at in the context of the wealthy, $100,000 is a very small number. A person with a billion dollars could spend $100,000 a day, every day, for over 27 years without running out of money. By providing $100,000 to each of the over 160 million Americans who currently have no wealth, the initiative aims to collectively move them to over $16 trillion in wealth.

The challenge in achieving this goal lies in how to get the funds to so many people. The first step is to make anyone with a Social Security number eligible to receive the funds. The next step is to encourage individuals, companies, organizations, and government entities to contribute to FY100 accounts by offering the most generous tax treatment for transfers of money into the accounts. This tax incentive is intended to encourage creative solutions for reaching over 160 million people and help them to build wealth.

It's worth noting that the initiative is not an easy task, and it's not without challenges. The initiative's goal is to reduce the gap between the rich and the poor, but it's a long-term goal that requires a lot of effort and resources.

Main Methods

▪ The Employed

Employed people are likely to be among the first to utilize FY100 accounts. The tax advantages for both them and their employer are greater than IRAs, 401(k)s, 403(b)s, 457s, and their Roth counterparts. The early use of FY100 accounts will come from the individuals who already use these savings vehicles. An employed 55-year-old who is already contributing the maximum to their 401(k) and their IRA using the catch-up provisions of each, would fund their own $100,000 contribution limit for an FY100 account in less than three years. The question becomes how they would next act.

Once the employed person's FY100 contribution limit is reached, they may help fund their spouse, thus putting assets into the spouse's name rather than as a beneficiary on their 401(k). Maybe they will help contribute to a child or other family members. With the very strong tax benefits, the desire to fund others FY100 accounts may be stronger than their desire to return to funding their 401(k)s like before. Each employed person will make different decisions, based upon their individual circumstances. An assumption is that those with more secure retirements would be encouraged to give further out in their networks.

▪ The Employer

Employers of for-profit companies and non-profit companies will have a very strong incentive to offer compensation to FY100 accounts. The ability to offset income and employment taxes will motivate them to explore every available method to compensate their employees with these funds, provided that employees are willing to accept them. Sharing of a portion of offset taxes will likely be a common practice, especially when employers want to encourage participation.

If an employee is hesitant to participate when $100 of their earned income is locked until they are 65, they may be more willing to do so if the $100 earned is matched with employer tax savings to $114 when directed to an FY100 account.

▪ The Business

When a business provides a service or sells a good, they are seeking to have a positive interaction with their customer. This may be done by providing a needed service or a quality product, however competition also leads the business to compete based on price as well. Businesses often use coupons, rebates, or other promotions to attract customers and incentivize them to choose that business's product or service.

Imagine a car dealership that typically offers a $1,000 rebate on the purchase of a vehicle. With the option of utilizing an FY100 account, the dealership has an opportunity to offer a rebate of $1,140 if the customer prefers to receive the rebate in their FY100 account. A grocery store that offers digital coupons displays coupon savings of $20 at the checkout register. A prompt would give the customer the opportunity to send $22.80 to their FY100 account instead of the deduction off of their bill.

What options could business provide when structuring a home loan or offering consulting services? Does an independent contractor such as a painter or landscaper offer you the opportunity to pay them in their FY100 account, instead of cash or a check made out to them? Will your electric co-op or the local credit union provide the best incentives using the FY100 account as a tool?

There are many opportunities at the consumer level for businesses and service providers to engage with their customers and benefit them with money going into their FY100 account and helping them on their way to the $100,000 contribution limit.

Other Methods

- ### The Government – Childhood Investment
Government has a vested interest in their constituents' financial security. Members of the community who are financially secure are less likely to look to government to support their basic human needs. There are lots of programs that are put out by federal, state, and local governments to support people with their health, housing, food, transportation, job training, retirement savings and more.

Instead of taxing and direct spending on these initiatives, some government leaders have explored ways to make small investments tied to individuals, which would grow over time using market forces. An example is a program that would establish a Baby Bond program which would provide every newborn with a savings account, funded by the government, that would be held in trust until the child reaches the age of 18. The account would be seeded with an initial deposit of $1,000 and would receive additional contributions from the government on an annual basis, based on the child's family income. The funds in the account could only be used for specific purposes, such as paying for higher education, purchasing a first home, or starting a small business.

With government leaders exploring options like this, expanding this concept to include FY100 accounts. If newborns were provided $1,000 in seed money from the government at the time of their birth, by the time the child reached 65, there would be over $44,000 in their FY100 account assuming a 6% reinvested dividend return.

If newborns were provided $100,000 in seed money from the government at the time of their birth, by the time the child reached 65, there would be over $4.4 million in their FY100 account assuming a 6% reinvested dividend return. Before discounting this idea as unfeasible, there are two numbers that should be considered.

The first number is how many children are born in the United States each year. There are over 3.6 million children born in the United States each year. Assuming that each one of these infants are provided an FY100 account with the full lifetime benefit contribution of $100,000, the government would need about $360 billion to fund this initiative.

The second number to know is how much the federal government spends on Social Security each year. Beginning in 2019 United States government began spending over $1 trillion per year on Social Security benefits. If the United States government could transition to investing in children at the time of birth, rather than providing a small income check to senior citizens, it would cost the federal government a third of what is spent on Social Security. The money invested in each infant would in turn help fund a robust public equity market for the benefit of domestic businesses. A healthy economy would return ample money for our seniors to live during their retirement years. This would also decrease the overall tax burden.

- **The Government – Business Bailouts**

There are times when the federal government may provide financial assistance to private businesses. This may be during an economic crisis, such as a recession or financial crisis and the government may provide financial assistance to businesses to prevent widespread job losses and economic instability. For example, during the 2008 financial crisis, the U.S. government provided bailouts to several large financial institutions, including AIG and Citigroup, to prevent their failure and mitigate the impact on the broader economy.

This may also take place in the aftermath of a natural disaster, such as a hurricane or earthquake, the government may provide financial assistance to businesses affected by the disaster to help them recover and rebuild. For example, after Hurricane Katrina devastated New Orleans in 2005, the government provided loans and grants to affected businesses.

In some cases, the government may provide bailouts to businesses that are critical to national security. For example, the U.S. government provided a bailout to General Motors in 2009, in part because the company's failure could have had significant negative consequences on the defense industry. Or the government may provide bailouts to businesses in specific industries that are facing significant challenges or crises. For example, the U.S. government provided bailouts to the airline industry after the 9/11 terrorist attacks, due to a sharp decline in air travel and many airlines faced bankruptcy. In some cases, the government may provide bailouts to businesses that face unforeseen circumstances that are beyond their control. For example, during the COVID-19 pandemic, the U.S. government provided financial assistance to businesses that were forced to close or significantly reduce their operations due to public health restrictions.

When these circumstances arise, there is an opportunity for the federal government to provide direct financial incentives to the effected businesses through the FY100 initiative. For instance, if a crisis is impacting a large domestic business that is publicly traded, instead of offering cash assistance or a loan, the federal government can fund the same amount of assistance through FY100 funding. This would involve allocating the funds evenly across FY100 accounts that have not yet reached their lifetime contribution cap. The bailout funds would then be directed from available FY100 assets to the affected company with repayment terms specified as a condition for receiving the funds.

This scenario would then provide more benefit than just the direct benefits of saving this critical company. Since the funds would be allocated to FY100 account holders, the money would be an investment that also builds wealth among the participants. The business would not just get free money, it would come with conditions that assured that the public dollars that were being used to rescue this business, but the business would be required to use the funds effectively for its long-term health. Ultimately, the funds would need to be repaid as the business successfully recovered. The use of the FY100 funds would be beneficial in that there is the opportunity to structure a very long time horizon that could meet the needs of the company in paying back the bailout funding. Depending on the terms negotiated by the federal government, there may also be a dividend accompanying the repayment of the principal.

- ## **The Government –Economic Development**

The federal government provides economic development investment or loans to businesses to promote job creation, support economic growth, and advance key national priorities such as technological innovation and environmental protection. The federal government provides economic development investment or loans to businesses in several ways, including loans and grants to small businesses to support their growth and development. The Small Business Administration (SBA) is the primary agency responsible for providing this support.

The government provides loans and grants to businesses located in rural areas to help promote economic development and job creation in these regions. The USDA Rural Development program is the primary agency responsible for providing this support. Businesses involved in infrastructure development projects, such as building highways, airports, and other transportation systems may also receive federal support through the Department of Transportation (DOT).

The federal government also provides loans and grants to businesses involved in technology development, such as research and development of new products or services. The National Institutes of Health (NIH) and the Department of Energy (DOE) are two of the agencies responsible for providing this support, specifically in the areas of public health and advancing national energy policies. Businesses involved in environmental protection projects, such as renewable energy or waste management may receive funding through the Environmental Protection Agency (EPA).

To facilitate job creation projects, such as manufacturing, construction, and tourism. The federal government through the Department of Commerce (DOC) and the Department of Labor (DOL) may fund loans or other incentive programs to meet national employment goals.

These examples illustrate how federal funding can flow directly to business. Although it involves public money going to non-governmental entities, the funding is justifiable because it helps achieve federal goals. As described with the federal bailout scenario above, FY100 funds can be used as an intermediary vehicle for financing the loan and other incentive programs offered by these federal agencies.

The federal funds could be directly distributed into the accounts of the FY 100 account holders who have not met their lifetime contribution caps. When providing financial incentives to businesses, repayment terms or profit-sharing agreements can be negotiated for each federal program. This investment not only meets the goals of the federal programs but also increases the overall funds available to FY100 account holders. This system reduces wealth inequality and serves other public goals, making it more beneficial for the public.

▪ The Game Show

Every day on television there are shows that bring everyday people into a studio to play a game in front of a televised audience. Many times, the game show is sponsored by products which may be won as prizes, or there are cash prizes available for the winners. Either the product sponsors or the producers of the game show may see the opportunity for larger prizes by offering the payouts into the contestant's FY100 account. At the time when a person may be winning a large windfall of prize money, people may choose the opportunity to secure their future, or some generous individuals may want to share their winnings with people in their life.

Some big game shows with huge audiences offer exceptionally large prizes to the winner at the end of the season. When the season is over, the winning contestant may walk away with a $1 million prize. Of course, the contestant may have to pay nearly 40% of those winnings in taxes, which can diminish the thrill of the prize.

Picture a different end to the game, where the host offers the winner $1.2 million to be distributed into FY100 accounts. That would certainly be an attractive offer to the winner, when so much more money could be claimed. Since there is a $100,000 lifetime cap on contributions to an FY100 account, imagine the compelling television moment as the winner shares the names of a dozen or more people in their life with whom they would choose to share the winnings.

▪ The Lottery

This section will not delve deeply into the merits or the harms of a statewide lottery. It is acknowledged that the purpose of these public lotteries is to raise money that funds government services without having to impose a tax. For those that play the lottery, the games themselves are a form of wealth redistribution. Often people who are less secure financially will purchase lottery tickets, and their money is concentrated and given out to make a few people wealthy.

Picture a scenario where the state lottery seeks to use its games to redistribute wealth into their residents' FY100 accounts. To better achieve the call of creating wealth for those that are less financially secure, the State does not collect proceeds from the FY100 games to fund government services. Instead, after costs the funds are all redistributed into prize money that is paid into FY100 accounts.

A good game could be a $100,000 scratch off ticket. The lottery officials are good at setting the odds in scratch off games, and the winning prize can be $100,000 going into FY100 accounts. If the winner of the scratch off already has $14,000 deposited into their FY100 account, they may choose to put $86,000 into their account, and distribute the remaining $14,000 to someone else. Some may choose to distribute the winnings in a different manner. The incentives and flexibility of FY100 accounts allows the winner to do as they please.

There could be a wide variety of games created, with different prize amounts, that could go towards FY100 accounts. In regular lottery games, there are no restrictions that would prevent a millionaire from winning a multi-million-dollar prize in the lottery. The difference with FY100 lottery games is that no prize would be able to exceed $100,000 going to one person, as the lifetime contribution limit to this type of account would prevent it.

This does not mean that lottery officials could not structure games with large prize drawings. For example, a drawing game that would have a $5 million FY100 account prize. When the prize is won, the winner of the $5 million would get to choose 50 or more people that the prize is distributed among. The lottery officials could have a program produced to distribute the winnings among the fifty or more people as chosen by the draw game's winner. That could be very heartwarming television.

■ The Charity

Charitable giving in the United States is significant with approximately three-quarters of giving coming from individuals. Considering that there is nearly $500 billion in annual giving each year, Americans are very generous, considerate, and cooperative people that freely give of themselves to help others.

Charitable giving in the United States covers a wide range of causes and organizations, including education, health, the arts, environmental causes, and social services. Many people choose to donate to charities that align with their personal values and interests. One of the larger categories of giving is Human Services with over 15% of total giving. People who give to Human Services give to organizations that provide services to meet the basic needs of individuals and families, such as food banks, shelters, and organizations that support children, the elderly, and people with disabilities.

People who give in this category, or even those that give to health, religion, or education may find it desirable to give directly to individuals through their FY100 account. By giving to organizations that have a 501(c) tax status, people can extend their ability to gift with the tax benefits. Since with the FY100 accounts, the tax benefits accrue to both the receiver and directly to the giver, people donating may find some utility to direct giving to individuals. Their giving would be very clear regarding who receives the gift, and not need a great deal of research into the organized charity, its mission, and how its board and staff deliver on its mission. Further, direct giving to an individual would remove the portion of giving reserved for the administrative and overhead costs of the organized charity.

For charities themselves, depending on their mission, they may find that FY100 accounts are a useful tool in delivering on that mission. For those working with the homeless or the impoverished, the individuals they serve may be unbanked, meaning without access to traditional banking services. Depositing funds into the FY100 account of a senior in need could be a central place to ensure the money given is going to the right person and does not get lost. Resources could be allocated for the individual's future, and money given now would grow over time.

For organized charities looking to help those with physical impairments, they may be concerned about their care in their senior years, when there is less concern when they are younger and in the care of their parents.

An education centered charity may look for a way to build wealth in families, which allows them to pass on generational wealth, which could assist in funding education for subsequent generations.

- **The Gambler**

This section will not delve deeply into the merits or the harms of gambling. It is acknowledged that many governments permit casinos, sports betting, and other forms of gambling to collect tax money that fund government services without having to impose a tax directly on their citizens. For those that gamble the wagers themselves are a form of wealth redistribution. Often people who are less secure financially will gamble, and their money is concentrated and given out to make a few people wealthy. In large respects the ones getting wealthy are the owners of the casinos and other gambling ventures.

For the owners of casinos and other gambling enterprises, they understand the margins of their business. They know that when people come in to bet, they are looking for reasonable odds of winning the prize for the bet they made. They know that when they give those payouts, people will continue to wager their money and the volume of money moving through their business increases. Gambling establishments profit from thin margins that benefit the house. To make their business more profitable, they want gamblers to place more wagers and push more money through their games.

These gambling establishments pay taxes on their profits, sometimes at a different scale than other businesses, however they too could benefit by giving payouts to an individual's FY100 account. The gambling establishment could afford to have higher payouts on FY100 games and wagers, provided the tax benefit on their profits. Likewise, the person making the wagers would not owe tax on their gambling winnings. This would result in a greater return on the games when they win. The concession for gamblers is that their winnings would not be immediately accessible through their FY100 account. Instead, they would have to wait until they turn 65 to access their winnings.

Casinos could set up designated machines and tables, whose payouts would be to FY100 accounts. Picture a video poker terminal that pays out to FY100 accounts. The gambler would have their Social Security number associated with their gaming card. When the gambler finishes their gambling session on the FY100 designated terminal, their winnings would be automatically transferred into their FY100 account, which is associated with their Social Security number.

Like lotteries, there would not be anything that would prevent prizes or winnings from exceeding the lifetime cap on the FY100 account. If a $1 million prize were won, the winner could choose to distribute the prize among 10 or more people, up to the lifetime cap on the FY100 accounts.

- **The Billionaires**

The options for billionaires and other ultra-high net worth individuals are certainly greater than most people for utilizing FY100 accounts. Even though the benefits of using FY100 accounts are extremely strong, the structure of FY100 accounts proves to have very limited personal value for those with very high net worth.

The same $100,000 lifetime contribution cap applies to everyone, so once the wealthy put in $100,000 to their own FY100 account, in order to take advantage of more tax benefits, they must distribute their money to others. They will have reached their personal contribution cap, and will not be able to receive any more, unless they are a beneficiary to someone else's FY100 account, and that person dies. Even with the earnings on the money, since the dividends are distributed equally across all FY100 account holders, the wealthy individual's account will grow at the same rate as everyone else.

As an employer, owner of a business, or serving on a charity, the wealthy have the same abilities as described above to benefit from the tax advantages of FY100 accounts. Of course, those advantages are as someone distributing money to others. It will be attractive to the wealthy, the same as others, to reduce tax liability by directing money to others' FY100 accounts.

If a wealthy person wants to limit the tax liability on $1 billion worth of their assets, they would be able to do that. To achieve that, they would need to direct $100,000 each to 10,000 different people. Or if they were directing $50,000 each, they would need to identify 20,000 different people to be recipients.

If the wealthy individual had 10,000 employees that they wanted to do that with, in the first year all of those employees would reach their $100,000 lifetime contribution cap. From their top executives to their line employees, no one would be able to receive any more. Assuming they wanted to do that again with another $1,000,000,000 in profit the second year, it would be harder for them to do.

Since their 10,000 employees all reached the cap the year before, they would need to look for new people. They would have new employees hired since the prior year, who did not reach the cap. There may be spouses, children, or other employee family members that their employees could direct the funds to. In short, the wealthy individual would need to expand their reach in order to achieve the same tax benefit.

Each year, the wealthy individual would be incentivized to decrease their tax liability by funding FY100 accounts. Each year that they do that, they need to push further and further away from the concentration of people near them. The lifetime contribution cap assures that this will happen. With hundreds of billionaires and other very wealthy people having signed on to the Giving Pledge, there are billions and billions of dollars that they have already planned to give away. Why not $100,000 at a time to lots of different people.

▪ Billionaire Challenge
In the United States there are almost half a million children who are

either orphans or in the foster care system. Through no fault of their own these children are starting life with obstacles that are not typically experienced by other children.

With so many ultra-high net worth individuals having signed on to the Giving Pledge, it should be readily attainable for America's billionaires to meet the FY100 Children Challenge. The challenge, proposed through this book, is to raise and distribute $50 billion among America's orphaned and foster children. Each child's FY100 account would be fully funded at $100,000, and their accounts will grow for the next 45 or more years.

If America's billionaires collectively have a net worth around $4.5 trillion the FY100 Children Challenge would amount to about 1.1% of their collective wealth. In some respects, 1% can be viewed as a significant amount in the context of all of the potential avenues for charitable giving, however this single challenge would positively impact almost two decades of orphaned and foster children. Don't forget, the billionaires would be able to take advantage of the tax incentives for their $50 billion in contributions. That would certainly partially offset the impact. Plus, many would see those funds come right back to their publicly traded domestic businesses in available FY100 funds to borrow.

While the direct benefit may take decades to materialize for these children, as they start their careers and begin their own families, some of the pressure for needing to save for their retirement may be lessened. It is an indirect benefit for helping these children early in their lives, but an impactful one as they head into their senior years and have a foundation for building a family legacy that may last generations.

5

FY100 - IMPACTS

The Fund Your Hundred initiative's impact on income and employment taxes will be closely examined, as it is assumed that it will have a significant effect on federal revenue. However, this assumption may not necessarily be accurate. This initiative has the potential to not only positively impact the flow of money, but also add stability and strength to the American economy. By encouraging people, companies, organizations, and government to give to individuals with FY100 accounts through tax incentives, it can increase the amount of money circulating in the economy. Additionally, by increasing the wealth of a large portion of the population, it will eventually lead to increased consumer spending, which in turn can boost economic growth.

Federal Government Taxes

There are four principal areas where federal taxes will be impacted by contributions to FY100 accounts. First will be corporate income taxes. By not assessing taxes to corporate income for funds going into an FY100 account, corporations are encouraged to transfer funds from the corporate entity to individuals. There are two impacted employment taxes, Medicare and Social Security. Each of these taxes fund services primarily benefiting the senior population. The funds going into FY100 accounts will primarily benefit this demographic. The fourth is individual income taxes, and like the corporate income taxes, this will encourage participation of individuals to save into an age restricted investment.

It is important to note that pulling these funds from tax collections does not remove the money from the economy. In fact, it activates all of the tax funds into a dynamic area of the economy, which can have strong economic benefits. With a clear picture of how money moves through an economy, you can see that these funds are removed for just one cycle of taxation, then are immediately put back into the flow of money where it is again subject to taxation by the federal government.

When money is put into FY100 accounts it includes a person's investment and also the income and employment taxes deferred from one cycle of the flow of money. Those funds are quickly available for publicly traded domestic companies to use the money to invest in equipment, purchase commodities, engage business services, and pay workers. Businesses will use these funds to operate their businesses, and the funds used will generate fiscal returns that return dividends to the FY100 account holders. By quickly putting these funds back into business, the funds then become subject to the corporate income taxes, employment taxes, and personal income taxes of the business' employees.

This money is used to pay for the equipment and everyone who is employed to make that equipment. It is used to pay for commodities and everyone who is employed to produce and deliver those commodities. It is used to provide business services and everyone who is employed to deliver those business services. This is not a withdrawal of capital from the economy to avoid taxation, it is the opposite. This is the activation of capital in the economy, which stimulates the flow of money through the economy and creates new opportunities for federal taxation through investment.

Let's look at a small-scale example of the flow of money through the economy. Ms. Wyl receives her paycheck one week in January, but she directs $1,000 to go into her FY100 account. She would have paid income tax on that $1,000 in April, but instead all of that money in her FY100 account is used by a publicly traded domestic business. It pays for new equipment from a business that manufactures the equipment needed by the company using the FY100 funds. The equipment manufacturer purchases the commodities it needs from a different company, who in turn hires trucking and other business services it requires to fulfill their commodity orders. Every one of these businesses is paying employees to conduct the work needed for their business. Every one of these businesses is creating new opportunities for generating corporate income, which will be subject to taxation, as well as employment compensation, which will be subject to employment and income taxation. How many cycles through the economy could these funds go through, and be subject to new taxation in the period from January to April, when Ms. Wyl was holding on to her tax payment.

Flow of Money Comparison

Let's examine two similar scenarios with different impacts on the flow of money. First, let's consider Mr. Efm who is paid by his employer every other Friday. He has been planning to have a painter come into his home and paint several of the interior walls. He has already purchased the paint and has a family friend who is a painter interested in doing the work. He was going to call to get the work started on Saturday when he was home and walk the painter through what he needed done. Instead, Mr. Efm was feeling quite ill and did not schedule the work for that weekend. Mr. Efm was unable to work for the next couple of weeks due to his illness, however, once he was feeling better, he called the painter to begin the work two weekends later.

In the second scenario, Mr. Efm did not fall ill and had the painter come to his home the first weekend. The painting work took three days and Mr. Efm paid the painter at the end of the day on Monday. Work had been slow for the painter, so he was glad to have had the work. He really needed some maintenance on his car, so he brought the car into the repair shop on Tuesday and the work was completed that day.

The repair shop owner used the money from the painter to pay for the part needed for the painter's car and had money to hire a landscaper to do work at his home that weekend. The landscaper had one person helping him, whom he paid. After the weekend, the landscaper called a friend of his, who is a painter, and had him come over that week to paint two rooms in his house.

These two simple situations show how the flow of money through the economy can have different levels of impact over the course of two weeks. In the first, the pay coming from Mr. Efm's employer only touched Mr. Efm and the painter. In the second the money moved faster through the economy, and because Mr. Efm activated it faster, in addition to the money reaching the painter, it reached a repairman, a parts supplier, a landscaper, the landscaper's helper, and back again to the painter. The same money had a larger impact because it was activated and moved quickly through the economy.

For the federal government, in the first scenario there was only income generated and eligible for tax from Mr. Efm and the painter. In the second scenario, it had five more instances to be subject to federal taxation. Bringing this concept back to someone contributing to an FY100 account, you can see that even if one cycle of income tax is missed, the federal government has many more opportunities to tax the money as it moves through the economy, especially if it is put into an active part of the economy and moves quickly.

Activated Economy

When money is put into FY100 accounts it is not going toward just any investments. The very nature of the investment is directed to the active parts of the American economy and is designed to deliver a stable investment which generates a reliable return on capital.

Funds in FY100 accounts are invested in domestic companies that seek their working capital from publicly traded equity markets. The money is used to purchase a new class of stock called FY shares. These stock shares are not subject to value fluctuations, as their base value is fixed. Instead, the capital appreciation comes from a dividend which is reinvested into the FY shares.

Companies that enter the public equity markets often do so in order to raise additional working capital. This capital may be used to expand production, enter new markets, or do other business activities that will generate a return on the investment for the business' owners and investors. The shares offered by the company for sale reflect the capital needs. In order to attract investors, the stock may promise a dividend on each share of stock, and the stock may also appreciate in value as the stock attracts additional investors.

By limiting the shares in FY100 accounts to FY shares, the accounts only earn reinvested dividends and are not subject to stock value fluctuations. Companies that provide dividends on stocks are often focused on the long-term performance of their company and make capital investments that deliver consistent and long term returns for their investors. Dividend producers add stability to the public equity markets and help to reduce volatility in the markets. Business often values stable markets, since they provide consistency and predictability which benefits their business decisions in deploying and activating their capital.

As domestic companies that are looking to return a dividend, their investments in equipment, commodities, business services, and labor will be focused in the United States more than their international business counterparts. This benefits the federal government by activating the domestic economy and providing other opportunities for taxation as money flows through the economy. Since these businesses are looking to provide a dividend return on the invested capital, they are incentivized to deploy the capital quickly, so it can begin generating returns for the business and its investors.

United States Government Encourages Corporate Investments

While FY100 investments may remove a cycle of income and employment taxes from the flow of money through the economy, there are many other examples of how the government promotes investment in business through favorable tax treatment.

The first example is with the 20% tax rate on long-term capital gains. Short-term taxes would be owed for gains on investments held less than a year. The 20% rate on long-term capital gains is a more favorable rate than the corporate income tax rate and a substantial portion of individual income taxes. This favorable treatment is commonly seen in executive compensation where the package offered has a limited amount of ordinary salary and benefits, but completes the compensation package with stock that can be sold under conditions later. The stock, when sold, is at a lower tax rate on the capital gains, rather than being ordinary income.

Ordinary investors can take advantage of the same tax treatment through their investments. This favorable tax rate on long-term capital gains signals the importance that the federal government places on money that is placed in the hands of businesses for their capital needs.

The next example is retirement investments. IRAs, 401(k)s, 403(b)s, 457s and related instruments can be invested in with pre-tax dollars. This means that to encourage Americans to invest in their retirement, the federal government is willing to forgo tax collection on the income used to purchase these investments. Further, the government will collect no tax on these funds for decades, until the investments are sold and capital gains taxes are due. A person who invested in these retirement saving vehicles beginning in their teenage working years would not be paying any tax on the proceeds for 40 years or more. During that entire period, the money is being used in the economy, and is flowing to various parts of the economy and generating taxes through the activated flow of money.

While the federal government is forgoing the front end of taxes on these retirement investments, the Roth versions of these have a counterpoint. People who invest in a Roth IRA, for example, will pay taxes on their initial investment. Those funds will then grow tax free over the coming decades.

The same activity happens with the invested money flows through an activated economy and benefits tax payers every time it is used. The other side to Roth investments is that the federal government is forgoing the backend taxes on the retirement account's proceeds at the time of withdrawal.

Whether a Roth or a traditional account, the federal government is forgoing one half of the investment where it could be collecting taxes. This shows the benefit that the federal government sees in not only encouraging people to save on their own for retirement, but that the money is activated in the economy while invested.

The federal government does not see this as an unlimited benefit, however. IRAs are limited to only those who have earned income, and for just a few thousand dollars each year. 401(k)s, 403(b)s, 457s are not only limited to those with earned income, but also only to those whose employer is sponsoring a plan. The funds in those investment plans have maximum employee contribution amounts, which are over $20,000 per year. While all of these may be invested for decades, the time of investment is limited. Account holders must begin taking distributions from the accounts at defined ages.

FY100 Accounts Supplement Existing Retirement Saving Options

The investments in FY100 accounts have a separate set of benefits and constraints from existing retirement saving options to better meet the goals of the initiative. The first significant difference is that anyone with a Social Security number can have and invest in an FY100 account. There is no requirement for a person to have earned income to participate. This means employed, unemployed, adults, and children can benefit from an FY100 account. Since tax benefits can be earned by someone contributing money to another person, a recipient does not need to have income to have an FY100 account. A person who gives money to another is not required to have a Social Security number.

Over 40% of American households do not have any retirement savings. While there are many reasons that contribute to this, part of the reason is that about half of American workers do not have access to an employer sponsored retirement plan, like a 401(k). Even when a person may have access to these plans, about a third of those who do choose not to participate.

FY100 Withdrawals

Another difference between FY100 and other retirement saving options is the age at which funds could be used. In an FY100 account the funds are locked until the account holder turns 65. There are no provisions to allow for early withdrawal. Compare this to other retirement savings plans which allow withdrawals as early as age 59 and a half, or Social Security that has an early benefit age of 62. These retirement plans may also have provisions for early withdrawal in the case of hardships, or with a tax penalty. The FY100 account is mostly intended to be for retirement, which is why all of its funds unlock at age 65, giving the account owner complete flexibility with how they use the money once unlocked.

The tax benefits are better than those of any other retirement savings vehicle and the fixed withdrawal time also provides certainty to the stock issuers that the funds will not be withdrawn early. The FY100 account is not intended to be used as emergency savings, insurance for illness or injury, or any other purpose before age 65. Other financial tools should be used to meet those needs.

While there is no flexibility when funds are unlocked, there is tremendous flexibility in when the funds are spent once unlocked. There are no requirements that the account holder spend any of the money in the account. These funds may be used to help build wealth in a family, not just for an individual. An account holder may never have to spend any of the accumulated account balance. If that occurs, wealth transfer of unlocked funds will go to beneficiaries who may then use the unlocked funds for any purpose.

FY100 Beneficiaries

If the FY100 account holder passes away at age 79, they will pass the unlocked funds in the account to their heirs. The beneficiaries will receive their portion of the funds in their own FY100 accounts as unlocked assets, meaning they could use the funds at any time. Further, inherited funds do not count toward the $100,000 lifetime contribution limit of the beneficiary. So, if a person has contributed $50,000 to their FY100 account, when a beneficiary passes away, and leaves them $125,000 of unlocked funds in the heir's FY100 account, the heir may still contribute the remaining $50,000, up to their lifetime contribution amount. In this case, their $100,000 contribution plus its accrued dividends would unlock at the time they turn 65. The $125,000 of inherited FY100 balance plus its accrued dividends would be inherited as unlocked at the time of the transfer and available for use at any time.

There is a scenario where an FY100 account holder passes away before they turn 65. Let's assume that a person with an $86,000 FY100 account balance passes away at the age of 60, five years before their funds unlock. If the $86,000 is passed on to a 35 year old heir, they would now have $86,000 in funds, plus future dividends on the $86,000, with an unlock date in five years. This means, the $86,000 will accumulate five more years' worth of dividends, then unlock when the account holder is 40. Any contributions, plus dividends, that the 35 year old heir would have made for themself, or contribute in the future, would unlock when they turn 65.

If an FY100 accountholder wishes to bequeath their balance to an organization or a charity, they must first withdraw the funds from the FY100 account. FY100 funds may only be held by an individual; an organization or charity is not eligible to have an FY100 account. At the time of death, FY100 funds must be transferred to at least one heir with an FY100 account. The FY100 accounts are intended to benefit people, not businesses, organizations, or charities. Also, if a person wishes to give some of their FY100 funds to someone while they are still alive, they must withdraw the funds from the FY100 account. A living person may not transfer FY100 funds from their account into another person's FY100 account.

FY100 Contribution Limits

There are two ways in which a person may accumulate funds in their FY100 account. The first is through direct contributions from any person, company, organization, or government, up to the account holder's lifetime contribution cap of $100,000 which is locked until the account holder turns 65. The second is to be an heir. There is no limit to the amount of funds that may be accumulated as an heir from others' FY100 accounts, with the unlock date on those funds matching the date of birth of the benefactor, plus 65 years.

For an IRA there is an increasing, indexed amount of funds that may be saved annually. Let's say a working teenager begins to save $6,000 per year until they turn 65. Over their working years, they will have contributed $282,000 into their IRA, almost three times as much as can be contributed in the FY100 account. The big benefit to the FY100 is that a benefactor could contribute $100,000 at birth under the FY100 initiative, which would then earn dividends for 65 years. This is a stronger benefit than an IRA, where there must be earned income for the contribution to be made.

In 401(k), 403(b), and 457 accounts, employees may contribute over $20,000 per year, not including employer contributions. Let's say a working teenager begins to save $20,000 per year until they turn 65. Over their working years, they will have contributed $940,000 into their retirement account, almost ten times as much as can be contributed in the FY100 account.

The FY100 account has very strong incentives for people to contribute to their own accounts and the accounts of others, and it is treated very favorably as an investment to be passed on to heirs. It does not compete with other retirement savings options as a way to build large account balances. That is not the intent. The intent is to provide extraordinarily strong incentives to encourage those who are not saving for retirement now to begin to do so, and to encourage others to contribute on behalf of those who are unable to because of their low incomes or other challenging circumstances.

Stable Investments

The nature of FY100 accounts is to encourage the spread of wealth across society. It is not a structure that promotes competition resulting in some investors benefiting to a greater degree than others. As such, there is no choice of investments with an individual's FY100 account. Instead, the available invested dollars are made available to the companies who meet the investment criteria and dividend returns that are established by the Securities and Exchange Commission. All of the dividends earned are distributed and reinvested evenly across all account holders. If the average dividend returns 4%, then everyone who has an account will get four new shares for every 100 FY shares owned.

This structure adds to the stability of the investments in that individual investors are not shifting their investments continually, trying to chase higher returns. This does not mean that the investment mix does not change over time. Since the investments made are locked and cannot be withdrawn until the investor turns 65, the SEC would be able to offer a much longer guarantee of capital investment to businesses who agree to higher dividend payments.

For example, each year, the SEC would know how many funds are invested by 55 year olds, and know that they can guarantee those funds to the businesses seeking capital for ten years. Similarly, they know how many funds are invested by 25 year olds, and know that they can guarantee those funds to those seeking capital for forty years. The businesses seeking the capital for a longer guaranteed period may need to provide a higher dividend return in exchange for the continued use of the capital. Market forces will prevail with the offering of FY100 capital.

The SEC would be able to adjust the investment mix to respond to changes in available capital and the businesses seeking the funds. To ensure they can access the capital, businesses would need to bid with higher dividends per FY share. Businesses that fail to deliver on their dividend distributions would be subject to default processes and risk losing access to the capital or other regulatory measures that may be imposed by the SEC.

The companies that participate in public equity markets have already made the decision to be bound by the enhanced regulatory environment of the SEC, rather than investments in private equity. Companies that seek to fill their capital needs in this manner are familiar with the volatility that comes in the public equity markets. They could experience rapid shifts in capitalization when there are changes in the broader economy, within their industry, or at their company. Broad impacts to the United States economy could result in a sudden depreciation of the company's stock by 20% or more, even if it is not directly related to the business' individual performance.

Companies that access their capital through FY100 funds could assure their stability, even when the underlying performance of the economy is in question. This is of benefit to not only the individual company, but to the American economy as a whole. The more businesses there are which have stable access to working capital, the less likely they are to be negatively impacted by emotional or reactionary trends in the broader economy. Instead of being faced with a 20% stock value depreciation caused by a broader sell-off in the market, the business would not have to respond with sudden cuts in workforce, reductions in capital equipment, or slowing of commodity orders. If the underlying business stays stronger than the national economy as a whole, they would be better able to weather a downturn, thus benefiting the broader economy.

Some sectors that may find accessing capital through the FY100 system more attractive than the public equity markets would be utilities, financials, resource extraction, industrials, real estate, transportation and shipping, energy, and materials. These types of industries may place a higher value of the underlying stability and availability of their capital sources, thus avoiding other market fluctuations would be attractive.

6
FY100 - WEALTH

Wealth refers to the total value of all the assets that a person or household possesses, after subtracting any outstanding debts or liabilities. These assets can encompass a wide range of items, including cash, investments, real estate, and personal property. Wealth is often used as a measure of an individual's or household's financial health and can be a means of achieving financial independence and security.

Wealth can be accumulated through various means, such as saving and investing, receiving an inheritance, or acquiring assets through business or other ventures. Additionally, wealth can also be used as a source of income through investments or businesses. For example, an individual may invest their wealth in stocks or bonds, generating a steady stream of income from the dividends or interest paid on these investments. Or an individual might use their wealth to start or invest in a business, which can provide them with an additional source of income.

Wealth Inequality

The origins of wealth inequality in the United States can be traced back to the country's founding, when most of the wealth was held by a small group of wealthy landowners and slaveholders. As the country developed and industrialization took hold, wealth became more widely distributed, but it was still heavily concentrated in the hands of a small elite.

Over time, various economic and political forces have contributed to the widening gap between the rich and the poor in the United States. For example, the concentration of wealth in the hands of a few powerful industrialists during the Gilded Age, as well as the growth of corporate power and the decline of unions, have all contributed to increasing wealth inequality.

Some of the wealthiest industrialists in the United States during the late 19th and early 20th centuries were John D. Rockefeller, Andrew Carnegie, and Cornelius Vanderbilt. John D. Rockefeller was the founder of Standard Oil and is considered to be the wealthiest person in history. Andrew Carnegie was a steel magnate and philanthropist. Cornelius Vanderbilt was a prominent businessman and industrialist who made his fortune in railroads and shipping.

In recent decades, the trend of increasing wealth inequality has continued, with the various measures describing how a few of the wealthiest Americans now owning a disproportionate share of the country's wealth compared to the bottom half of Americans. The efforts to classify the disparity in wealth come in many forms. Some analyze individuals while others focus on households. Trying to measure wealth is also challenging, with some using homeownership, real estate, investments, retirement accounts, debt, collectibles, antiquities, or art. Some of these categories of wealth are difficult to identify and value for the sake of a comparison. Most often the comparison will identify a small group of very wealthy individuals and demonstrate that they hold more wealth than over half of Americans. A different way to look at this is that about half of Americans have no wealth, so anyone with some wealth, will have more than tens of millions of other people.

Despite efforts to address wealth inequality through progressive taxation and social welfare programs, the gap between the rich and the poor in the United States remains wide, with many Americans struggling to make ends meet while a small elite enjoys tremendous wealth and privilege.

The consequences of wealth inequality are far-reaching and can have a significant impact on people's lives. For example, studies have shown that wealth inequality can lead to poorer health outcomes, lower levels of social mobility, and increased political polarization.

So, why don't policymakers just tax the assets of the wealthy more and redistribute those assets to everyone else? There are many challenges with this which will be covered in the rest of this chapter. A main reason is that government primarily uses its tax receipts to provide services and income for disadvantaged people. Government provides medical services, housing assistance, food assistance, job training, retirement income, and other services and income at a point in time, meeting a current need of their constituents, not future needs. The federal government does not have programs to address wealth inequality or to redistribute wealth.

Efforts to Reduce Wealth Inequality

There are many different policy options that have been discussed and tried to reduce wealth inequality in the United States. Some of the most often discussed approaches include:

- Raise the minimum wage: Increasing the minimum wage would help to boost the incomes of low-wage workers, who are often disproportionately affected by wealth inequality.

  - The minimum wage in the United States has changed several times over the years. The federal minimum wage was first established in 1938 as part of the Fair Labor Standards Act (FLSA) at 25 cents per hour. It has increased multiple times over the years, with the most recent increase to $7.25 per hour in 2009. Some states and municipalities have their own minimum wage laws that are higher than the federal minimum wage. The main challenge to using a change to the minimum wage as a solution to wealth inequality is the conflation of income and wealth. Changes to income, particularly at the lowest end of the income scale translate most readily into new consumption. New consumption benefits the consumer with more goods; however, it also adds more wealth to those who own the means of production.

- Implement progressive taxation: Implementing progressive taxation, where those with higher incomes pay a higher percentage of their income in taxes, can help to redistribute wealth from the highest earners to those who are less well-off.

  - The United States Tax Code has undergone various changes over time and has become increasingly progressive in recent decades. Progressivity in a tax system refers to the fact that people with higher incomes pay a larger percentage of their income in taxes than those with lower incomes. One way in which the Tax Code has become more progressive is through the implementation of progressive income tax rates, where people with higher incomes are taxed at a higher rate than those with lower incomes. The top marginal income tax rate, which is the highest rate that people with the highest incomes pay, has been increased multiple times in the past century. Another way in which the Tax Code has become more progressive is through the creation of tax credits and deductions that benefit lower-income individuals and families. For example, the Earned Income Tax Credit (EITC) is a refundable tax credit that benefits people with low-to-moderate incomes who work. Progressive taxation has not resulted to changes in wealth distribution, primarily because of how tax dollars are spent. With over a quarter of federal dollars spent on health and over a quarter spent on the military, the federal budget is not spent on programs that translate to building wealth. Additional categories of federal spending include paying debt, veterans' benefits, unemployment, education, and more. While there is a couple percent going toward housing, the majority of that is supporting rental housing programs. These translate much more closely to consumptive categories of spending, and not ones that build wealth.

- Wealth taxes: Some countries have implemented wealth taxes, which are taxes on the total value of an individual's assets, including real estate, stocks, and savings. Wealth taxes can help to reduce income inequality by reducing the amount of wealth held by the wealthiest individuals.

- This is a slightly different approach than progressive taxation, which focuses on taxing income. By taxing wealth, the idea is to either decrease or slow the continued accumulation of wealth. Wealth taxes have been implemented in various forms throughout history, with the first recorded instance being in ancient Egypt. In more recent times, they have been used by countries such as France, Spain, and Switzerland. In the United States, a federal wealth tax has not been implemented since the 1920s. However, many states and municipalities have property taxes, which are a form of wealth tax on real estate. In addition to the new administrative burden that would come from the imposition of a wealth tax, many types of assets can be relocated and avoid the tax, unlike real estate. While a wealth tax would be a new revenue source for the federal government, there is no new program of spending that would be in place to reduce wealth inequality. The federal budget is not spent on programs that directly address wealth inequality.

- Provide universal access to education and training: Investing in education and training programs can help to increase the skills and knowledge of people in lower income groups, which can in turn help to increase their earning potential.

  - Access to education and increases in educational attainment in the United States have changed significantly over time. In the past, access to education was limited to a small portion of the population, primarily white, male, and wealthy individuals. However, over the past century, there have been significant efforts to expand access to education for all individuals, regardless of race, gender, or socioeconomic status. As a result, there has been a steady increase in educational attainment in the United States. In 1940, less than 10% of the population over the age of 25 had completed four or more years of college. By 2020, over 30% of the population over the age of 25 had completed four or more years of college. Additionally, the percentage of the population with a high school diploma or equivalent has increased from around 25% in 1940 to over 90% in 2020. Increased educational attainment has not resulted in a reduction in wealth inequality. While this educational attainment has assisted in shifting the economy from one with significant industrial production to a larger portion of workers in a knowledge economy, there remains a challenge in workers converting their income into wealth.

- Expand access to affordable housing: Providing more affordable housing options can help to reduce the burden of housing costs on lower-income households, freeing up more of their income for other expenses.

  - The federal government has provided affordable housing through a variety of programs over time. Some key examples include: The New Deal-era Federal Housing Administration (FHA), which provided insurance for mortgages, making it easier for low-income families to purchase homes. The National Housing Act of 1949, which created the Federal Housing Administration (FHA), the Federal National Mortgage Association (Fannie Mae), and the Federal Home Loan Mortgage Corporation (Freddie Mac) to provide funding for affordable housing. The Housing and Urban Development Act of 1965, which created the Department of Housing and Urban Development (HUD) and provided funding for public housing and community development programs. The Low-Income Housing Tax Credit program, which provides tax credits to developers who build or rehabilitate affordable housing. The Section 8 Housing Choice Voucher program, which provides vouchers to low-income families to help them afford housing in the private market. The government has also provided funding for homelessness prevention and affordable housing through Community Development Block Grants (CDBG) and HOME Investment Partnerships Program (HOME). In recent years, the government has also focused on increasing the availability of affordable rental housing through programs such as the National Housing Trust Fund, and the Capital Magnet Fund. While early federal programs had an emphasis on improving access to home loans, recent years have focused more on subsidizing rent. The challenge with providing programs that encourage building more rental units and subsidizing the rent for individuals, is that neither of those strategies assist in leading to home ownership and the accumulation of wealth that homeownership brings. The percentage of home ownership in the United States has fluctuated over time, but generally trended upward until the early 2000s. From the 1940s to the 1960s, the rate of home ownership consistently increased, reaching a peak of about 64% in the mid-1960s. The rate then fluctuated between 62% and 66% until the early 2000s, when it began to decline. The rate reached a trough of about 62% in 2016 before ticking back up to about 64% in 2020. The stagnation in the increase of homeownership indicates either a natural limit to the number of people seeking to own a home, or it demonstrates a barrier to increased home ownership that cannot be crossed.

- Increase access to affordable healthcare: Providing more affordable healthcare options can help to reduce the financial burden of healthcare costs on lower-income households.

- Prior to the implementation of the Affordable Care Act (ACA) in 2010 the way health insurance coverage was provided in the United States was mainly through employer-sponsored insurance, and many Americans who didn't have employer-sponsored insurance, had to purchase their own insurance with high cost and limited options. The percentage of Americans with health insurance coverage fluctuated. The U.S. Census Bureau reported that the percentage of Americans without health insurance coverage increased from 14.8% in 2000 to

16.7% in 2009. There are various factors that contributed to this increase in the percentage of uninsured Americans, such as job loss due to the economic recession, increased healthcare costs, and the lack of access to affordable health insurance coverage. Additionally, many employers stopped offering health insurance coverage to their employees, or reduced the number of employees covered. The ACA was aimed to help increase access to health insurance by expanding Medicaid and creating state-based health insurance marketplaces where individuals could purchase private health insurance with the help of government subsidies. After the ACA was implemented, the percentage of uninsured Americans decreased significantly. According to the U.S. Census Bureau, the uninsured rate dropped from 16.0% in 2010 to 8.9% in 2018, the lowest rate ever recorded. Even with the reduction in Americans without health insurance, there has remained a growing level of wealth inequality. Healthcare costs have tended to outpace inflation, the increase in health insurance coverage in recent years has not led to a noticeable impact for many families. Any savings that may have been realized by families for their health expenses has not translated into a noticeable increase in wealth for lower income Americans.

- Provide targeted assistance to low-income households: Programs such as welfare and food assistance can help to reduce the financial burden on lower-income households, allowing them to better meet their basic needs and potentially increasing their economic mobility.

  - Welfare and food assistance programs in the United States have undergone significant changes over time. In the 1930s, the federal government established programs such as the Federal Emergency Relief Administration and the Civilian Conservation Corps to provide financial assistance to individuals and families during the Great Depression. In the 1960s, President Lyndon B. Johnson's Great Society initiatives expanded the welfare system to include programs such as Medicaid, food stamps, and Head Start. The welfare system underwent significant changes in the 1990s under President Bill Clinton, with the passage of the Personal Responsibility and Work Opportunity Reconciliation Act, which placed time limits on welfare assistance and placed a stronger emphasis on work requirements for recipients. In recent years, there have been ongoing debates about the level of welfare and food assistance provided to Americans. Some argue that current levels are inadequate and that more resources are needed to help low-income individuals and families meet their basic needs, while others argue that the welfare system is overly generous and that more needs to be done to encourage self-sufficiency. The income requirements for welfare and food assistance vary depending on the program and the state in which you live. In general, these programs are intended for low-income individuals and families, and the specific income limits are often based on the federal poverty level (FPL). For example, in 2021, the FPL for a family of four is $12,880, and many states use this as a benchmark to determine eligibility for assistance programs. However, it can vary, and some states may have a higher or lower limit. Additionally, some states may have different limits for different programs. Programs that are put in place to meet the very basic needs of people are aimed at those with the lowest of incomes in the United States. While the programs may provide some levels of relief, they do not provide assistance to a level sufficient enough that the recipients total consumption needs are met. There is no evidence that people receiving these benefits are converting their other income into sustained wealth.

Income

Income refers to the money or salary that an individual or a household receives from various sources, such as employment, investments, and business ventures. This money can come in the form of wages, salaries, bonuses, commissions, and other forms of compensation for services rendered. Income can also be generated from non-work sources, such as rental properties, dividends from stocks, and interest from savings accounts. Income is an important measure of financial well-being and is used to determine a person's ability to afford things like housing, food, and other necessities. Ultimately, income is the flow of money that a person receives from any source. For most people the main source of income is their wages from work.

Income Inequality

The FY100 initiative is intended to address wealth inequality. Commonly in discussions about wealth inequality, the concept is often conflated with income inequality and discussions blur the lines between each. It is necessary to clearly distinguish between the two concepts in order to identify and address their respective solutions. In discussion of the challenges of income inequality people often bring up concerns about billionaire wealth. Although somewhat related, addressing one of these does not automatically resolve the other. It is important to note that while the FY100 initiative is not intended to directly address income inequality, that does not mean that income inequality is not an important issue. Separate solutions need to be put forward to address income inequality.

While having more income is certainly beneficial to the accumulation of wealth, there are scenarios of each where they do not relate. There are many people who have a high income; however their lifestyle is highly consumptive and they do not accumulate wealth proportionate to what their income could afford. If they live in an expense location, rent their home, and spend heavily on travel and experiences, even with a high income, they may not accumulate much wealth. Another case would be a person who had a high income and used that to accumulate wealth over time. When they retire, their income diminishes significantly, however they have retained a large amount of wealth. Their annual income tax return may show little in the way of income, yet they maintain millions of dollars' worth of assets that do not provide income, like primary and secondary homes.

A person with a modest income that invests in a home or equities could see their wealth grow if their home value appreciates considerably over time, or if they have success with the investments that they made. In this circumstance the wealth they accumulated may not be proportional to their income. Other scenarios, such as receiving an inheritance, winning a civil judgment, or winning the lottery, could result in significant wealth even if a person's income is relatively low. These situations are certainly not typical.

Income inequality in the United States has been a regular component of the nation's history, and there are many factors that contribute to it. Some of the origins of income inequality in the United States include:

- Historical and structural factors: Income inequality in the United States has roots in the country's history, including the institution of slavery and the exploitation of marginalized groups. These historical and structural factors have contributed to ongoing disparities in income.
- Education: Access to education has been viewed as a key factor in an individual's ability to earn a good income. In the United States, there are significant disparities in the quality of education that different people receive, which can contribute to income inequality.
- Employment and wages: Income inequality can be influenced by

the types of jobs that are available, as well as the wages that are paid for those jobs. In the United States, there are significant disparities in employment and wages.

• Government policies: Government policies can also play a role in income inequality. For example, tax policies that favor high earners or people in certain industries can contribute to income inequality.

Today, income inequality in the United States remains a significant issue. According to data from the U.S. Census Bureau, the top 1% of households in the United States earn about twenty times as much as the bottom 50% of households. Income inequality has increased over the past several decades.

There are many efforts underway to address income inequality in the United States, including policies that aim to improve access to education, increase the minimum wage, and provide financial support to low-income individuals and families. Many federal and state programs have been implemented to address income inequality; however the issue persists. This book is not intended to present an idea to address income inequality or debate the merits of these ideas to address income inequality. While income and wealth have some relationship to each other, the FY100 initiative is intended to present an idea for reducing wealth inequality, however not by only addressing income inequality.

Income and Wealth Inequality Differences

Income inequality refers to the unequal distribution of income among individuals or households in a population. It is often measured by comparing the income of different percentiles of the population, such as the top 1% versus the bottom 99%, or by calculating the ratio of the highest earners' income to the lowest earners' income in a company or between professions.

Wealth inequality, on the other hand, refers to the unequal distribution of wealth, or the total value of a person's assets, such as property, savings, and investments, minus their debts. Like income inequality, wealth inequality can be measured by comparing the wealth of different percentiles of the population or by calculating the ratio of the wealthiest individuals' wealth to the least wealthy individuals' wealth.

Income inequality and wealth inequality are often interrelated because a person's income can contribute to their wealth over time through saving and investing. For example, if a person has a higher income, they may be able to save more money and invest it in assets such as stocks or real estate, which can grow in value and increase their wealth. On the other hand, if a person has a lower income, they may have less disposable income available to save and invest, which can limit their ability to build wealth.

Additionally, wealth can also contribute to income through investment income, such as dividends or capital gains. For example, if a person has a large amount of wealth invested in stocks or other assets that generate income, they may have a higher income as a result. Not all wealth translates into income, like a primary residence which is typically not an income-generating asset. There is an opportunity for those with wealth to generate income, by selling their assets.

It is because of the income generating potential of wealth that can make it a more powerful force in one's economic life. When a person works, their income is attributable to the effort that they put in. When they stop working, the income they earned from their labor stops as well. With wealth, once accumulated, it can be used to generate income. If a person stops working, the wealth deployed to generate income does not stop. It can continue to generate income, so long as it is in an investment that can provide a financial return. Further, that wealth can be transferred to others. That is a quality not associated with most income. In some cases, income like pension or Social Security payments have survivor benefit provisions which may transfer income to a dependent under certain circumstances.

Overall, income inequality and wealth inequality are two separate but related concepts that reflect the unequal distribution of resources among individuals and households in a population.

Generational Wealth

Wealth has a tremendous power for the economic health of a family, and that lies with the potential for the wealth to persist and be passed from their original owner on to heirs. This is often called generational wealth and refers to the wealth that is passed down from one generation to the next within a family. It can include financial assets such as savings, investments, and real estate, as well as non-financial assets such as businesses and intellectual property.

There are several factors that can lead to the accumulation of generational wealth:

• Financial planning: Creating a financial plan and setting financial goals can help families make informed decisions about how to allocate their resources and build wealth over time.

•   Investing: Making smart investments in a diverse range of assets, such as stocks, bonds, and real estate, can help families grow their wealth over time.

•   Saving: Building up a savings cushion can provide a financial buffer in case of unexpected expenses or economic downturns, and can also help families invest in opportunities that may arise.

•   Education: Investing in education, both for oneself and for future generations, can lead to higher earning potential and better job opportunities, which can contribute to the accumulation of wealth.

•   Entrepreneurship: Starting and successfully running a business can be a lucrative way to build wealth, especially if the business is passed down to future generations.

•   Inheritance: Receiving a financial inheritance from a relative can provide a significant boost to a family's wealth.

•   Homeownership: Owning property, especially real estate, can be a source of wealth, especially if the property increases in value over time.

•   Debt management: Managing debt responsibly, including paying off high-interest debt and avoiding taking on unnecessary debt, can help families keep more of their income and build wealth over time.

•   Estate planning: Planning for the distribution of assets in the event of death can help ensure that wealth is passed down to future generations in an orderly and efficient manner.

Generational wealth, which refers to the practice of passing wealth down from one generation to the next, is often seen as a way to preserve and grow family wealth. However, this practice does not address the issue of wealth inequality. This is because, even though the wealth was accumulated by one person, when they pass away, they may choose to pass it on to a single heir rather than distributing it among a broader family or community. This can result in a concentration of wealth in the hands of a small number of individuals, rather than being distributed more broadly.

Furthermore, this practice may perpetuate systems of privilege, where wealth accumulation is not based on merit but rather on accident of birth. This can create a self-perpetuating cycle of wealth and privilege, where those who are already wealthy are more likely to remain wealthy, while those who are not wealthy are less likely to achieve wealth and upward mobility.

The Giving Pledge

According to Givingpledge.org, the Giving Pledge is a campaign to encourage the world's wealthiest individuals and families to commit to giving the majority of their wealth to philanthropic causes. The Giving Pledge was founded by Bill and Melinda Gates and Warren Buffet in 2010 and is administered by the Bill & Melinda Gates Foundation.

The Giving Pledge is not a legally binding contract, but rather a moral commitment to give back to society. The pledge is open to billionaires and multimillionaires from all countries and backgrounds, and those who take the pledge can choose to support any causes or organizations that align with their values.

According to Givingpledge.org, the goals of the Giving Pledge are to:

• Encourage philanthropy: The Giving Pledge aims to inspire more people to give back to their communities and make a positive impact on the world.
• Promote transparency: By publicly announcing their commitment to giving, pledge signatories can be held accountable for their philanthropic efforts and inspire others to do the same.
• Facilitate collaboration: The Giving Pledge encourages pledge signatories to collaborate with each other and share their experiences and insights on philanthropy.

As of 2023, the Giving Pledge has over 230 signatories from 28 countries. Some of the notable figures who have taken the pledge include Mark Zuckerberg, Elon Musk, Paul Allen, and Michael Bloomberg. With the passage of the FY100 initiative, there is an opportunity for the pledge's signatories to add another goal. The goal could be:

• Encourage Individual Giving: The Giving Pledge can directly benefit the lives of individuals by supporting the investment in their wealth, which can serve as a foundation for their family.

Billionaires

People look to the wealth that has been accumulated by billionaires and other ultra-high net worth individuals and see the inequality of wealth distribution in our capitalist society as unjust. There are often statistics or infographics which show the top x wealthiest Americans have more wealth than the bottom 50%. As presented in this light, the disparity in wealth is astounding. When so many have none, and so few have unimaginable wealth, an immediate reaction is to think of how to take that wealth and redistribute it. Tax the wealthy. Eat the rich.

If we could wave a wand and get the least wealthy half of Americans $100,000 in retirement funds available to them from the wealthiest Americans, that would amount to over $16,000,000,000,000. One hundred thousand dollars is a relatively modest amount of wealth, but would mean so much for those that don't have any today. It could enable higher education, a down payment on a home, or even just relief from accumulated debts.

There is one significant problem with this idea. America's billionaires do not have seventeen trillion dollars between them to either tax or take. The politicians, activists, and advocates who peddle the ideas of taxing or taking sufficient resources from billionaires are delivering nothing but false hope.

It is difficult to get an accurate account of the wealth of billionaires, since not all of their assets are publicly known or valued. Many of their assets also fluctuate significantly with the economy and their individual investment choices, as they often hold significant amounts of publicly traded securities. Combined, billionaires hold less than $5 trillion in assets. Even if every asset of billionaires was liquidated, that would not even translate to $100,000 for a third of the least wealthy Americans.

Another way to look at it, billionaires liquidated wealth would only amount to about $15,000 per American. Meanwhile many of the largest businesses in the United States would see huge amounts of their operating capital vanish. For the people who propose a 2% wealth tax on billionaires, that would generate about $100 billion annually. That is about $300 per American per year.

Wealth taxes may sound good to an activist, but they do not amount to much when distributed across the immense population of Americans. The billionaires just are not wealthy enough for a wealth tax to matter. That is a strange and counterintuitive statement. From the perspective of most Americans, billionaire wealth is unfathomable. From the context of over 330 million Americans, it just is not that much money.

The wealth of billionaires is mostly illiquid. Those assets are often deployed as working capital in their businesses or other investments, land, or other physical or not readily transferred assets. To take those funds and redistribute them would mean pulling hundreds of billions of active capital from American businesses and the divestiture of significant land assets. If the sale of those stocks and land were to be compelled, where would the money come from for the assets to be purchased, to pay that tax?

The number of billionaires in America keeps changing, but it has generally trended to an increase of billionaires over time. According to Americansfortaxfairness.org, in April 2021, U.S. billionaires had an estimated wealth of $4.5 trillion. With large stock market losses in 2022, many billionaires saw significant losses of wealth, as did many retail investors with modest portfolios. A strengthening economy would see billions in wealth flooding back to billionaires due to their positions as the owners of industry in America.

Billionaire FY100 Children's Challenge

American billionaires could participate in an FY100 challenge. In the United States there is just under half a million children who are either orphans or are in the foster care system. The FY100 challenge would be for American billionaires to work together to fund $50 billion dollars of FY100 contributions which will give every orphan and foster child in America $100,000 in their FY100 account. These funds will be able to grow over the decades of their life and provide a level of security in their retirement that they may not have had as children. This is described more under the Creative Distribution chapter.

UBI

Earlier in this chapter there was discussion of the differences between income inequality and wealth inequality. While they are distinct, one area of addressing income inequality has gotten significant attention in recent years. Universal Basic Income (UBI) is a proposed policy that would provide a regular, unconditional cash payment to all members of a society, regardless of their income or employment status. The attention to this is often conflated with billionaire wealth as basis to provide a UBI. This section is not intended to provide a full analysis of UBI, but to provide some basic perspective of what it is and why there is a significant challenge to implementation. Ultimately, increasing incomes with a UBI would likely not address wealth inequality. The main objectives of UBI are to:

• Reduce poverty: UBI aims to provide a basic level of income to everyone, which can help to reduce poverty and increase financial security.

• Foster economic independence: By providing a regular source of income, UBI can enable people to pursue opportunities and make choices that align with their values and goals, rather than being forced to take low-paying jobs just to make ends meet.

• Promote social equality: UBI can help to reduce income inequality and promote social equality by providing a basic level of income to everyone, regardless of their income or employment status.

There are several different approaches to implementing UBI, including:
•	Direct cash transfers: One common proposal of implementing UBI is through direct cash transfers, where the government provides a regular cash payment to all citizens or residents of a country.
•	Negative income tax: Another approach is a negative income tax, where individuals or families with low incomes receive a cash payment from the government to bring their income up to a certain level.
•	Reducing bureaucracy: Some proponents of UBI argue that it could be funded by reducing bureaucracy and inefficiencies in existing social welfare programs.

One of the more common proposals for universal basic income is a $1,000 check per month for every adult. With about 260 million adults in the United States, this would cost approximately $3.1 trillion per year. For those favoring to tax the billionaires, their wealth would be completely exhausted in less than two years under this UBI scenario. For those looking to apply the additional taxes in a progressive manner across the population, the current federal budget is about $4 trillion. This would mean at least a 75% increase in federal tax receipts across taxpayers.

Most funds distributed through a UBI would be used for consumption expenses. While this will generate additional economic activity, it will certainly be inflationary as well. Looking at recent examples, Federal pandemic fiscal incentives through the CARES Act and ARPA led to trillions of dollars delivered directly to individuals, businesses, and governments. Economic data shows that it did lead to significant consumptive spending, which reverberated through the economy creating delays in manufacturing, distribution and logistics challenges, corporate profit taking, and inflationary effects.

Those effects were heavily influenced by the rising unemployment that preceded the stimulus actions, pandemic responses, and major global geopolitical challenges. The impacts of new income programs would certainly manifest itself differently under current circumstances, however, as with the nature of most Americans income today, much of that income would be used in a consumptive manner. Of course, the profits of the increased consumption would primarily go to those who own the sources of production in society today. This would further exacerbate wealth inequality. This is because there would be no change in the ownership of the means of production. The FY100 initiative begins to shift more of the ownership of the means of production into more Americans hands. As those businesses profit and yield dividends, so will those invested in the FY100 accounts.

Baby Bonds

According to legislation on Congress.gov, in 2021, legislation was introduced called the "American Opportunity Accounts Act" that would establish a baby bond program in the United States. The program would provide every newborn in the country with a savings account, funded by the government, that would be held in trust until the child reaches the age of 18. The account would be seeded with an initial deposit of $1,000 and would receive additional contributions from the government on an annual basis, based on the child's family income. The funds in the account could only be used for specific purposes, such as paying for higher education, purchasing a first home, or starting a small business.

The goal of the baby bond program was described as a means to reduce income inequality and provide children from low-income families with a financial foundation that will help them achieve economic mobility. It was argued that such a program would help level the playing field for children from disadvantaged backgrounds, who may not have the same financial resources or opportunities as those from more affluent families.

As proposed, the program is described as one that reduces income inequality. I contend that while it is small in scale it may look like a means to address income inequality, it is proposed to function more like the FY100 initiative, in that it builds wealth. A small asset is the starting point, but it grows over the next 18 years to provide a modest asset that would assist with education, home ownership, or to support entrepreneurism. As described, it appears to be a program to provide a modest amount of wealth to help achieve big goals, not just a program to supplement income.

Three key differences between the baby bond program and FY100 are the permitted participants, source of funding, and the means of asset growth. First, the baby bond program was proposed to only benefit those with low income, where FY100 is open to all, with a lifetime contribution cap.

The baby bond program is recommended to be funded by the government through general taxation. Compared to the FY100 which is incentive by government, but ultimately funded through capital enterprises. The baby bond assets grow through traditional market investments, and continued government investment, while the FY100 utilizes investment initiated by qualifying capital seekers. With a couple small changes in approach, a baby bond program could more closely resemble the FY100 initiative.

7

FY100 - LENSES

With the introduction of a novel concept or a new idea, there is a natural inclination to want to assess that idea. It is important to test and examine to assure that the idea can withstand a variety of scrutiny. In the event the idea, or a portion of it is successfully challenged, the idea will need to evolve and adapt, ensuring the core of the idea can rise above the challenges and meet its goals.

When someone tests an idea, often they examine the idea through a particular lens that informs their way of thinking. For Fund Your Hundred accounts, people may test the idea through various economic lenses. It may be based on a particular economic philosophy or even from a micro or macro viewpoint. For FY100 accounts to exist as described in this book, there is a need for a regulatory change, particularly in the tax code. As such, the people responsible for adopting the new regulations would be examining FY100 accounts through political lenses as well. This chapter seeks to view FY100 through many of these lenses. In crafting the FY100 initiative, I sought to be applicable to them all.

As you apply your own critical lens to the idea for FY100 accounts, assure that you think through the perspective and test it within its subject. Don't look at FY100 accounts and conclude it would not work because it 'won't bake bread'. That is acknowledged, as the idea is not intended to 'bake bread'. Test FY100 about its merits, not tangential issues. For example, FY100 accounts are intended to reduce wealth inequality, not income inequality, not access to healthcare, nor home ownership. While reducing wealth inequality may be tangential to these and others because they are fiscal in nature, just because you can use FY100 funds to buy flour, butter, and eggs does not mean that it can 'bake bread'.

The Invisible Hand

When Adam Smith looked across the enriching landscapes of rural Kirkcaldy, he also saw the developing industrial scene of a 19th century seaport and contemplated how its economy functioned. His writings inspired the study of modern economics. While his work was very broad, one of the concepts that resonated in his writings was the phrase the Invisible Hand. The phrase was first coined by Smith in his book "The Wealth of Nations". In the context of the book, the Invisible Hand refers to the idea that individuals pursuing their own self-interest in a free-market economy can, through competition and trade, bring about an outcome that is beneficial to society as a whole. Smith argued that, through the Invisible Hand, market forces could lead to the most efficient allocation of resources and the greatest overall prosperity for society.

The concept of the Invisible Hand was later developed and elaborated upon by influential mid-20th century economists. This version of the Invisible Hand was based on the idea that the market is inherently efficient and that government intervention in the economy is generally unnecessary or even harmful. According to this view, the Invisible Hand of the market is capable of achieving optimal outcomes without the need for government intervention.

The concept of the Invisible Hand has been the subject of much debate, and many economists do not fully subscribe to either Adam Smith's original vision or the version espoused by mid-20th century economists. Some argue that the Invisible Hand is not always able to produce optimal outcomes and that government intervention is necessary in certain circumstances. Others argue that the Invisible Hand is simply a metaphor and may not accurately reflect the complexity of real-world economic systems.

▪ The Clumsy Hand and The Greedy Hand

The United States economy is often referred to as being guided by the Invisible Hand, a metaphor used to describe the unseen forces that drive economic growth and prosperity. However, for many Americans, this metaphor has not accurately reflected reality. Instead of benign results that happen unintentionally, the economic landscape in the US has been shaped by a complex set of rules, policies, and decisions that are often out of view and difficult for the average person to understand.

One example of this is the tax code, which can be challenging for most people to navigate, let alone understand its nuances. There are different tax rates for individuals and businesses. Some economic activity is viewed in a tax favorable light, while other activity is discouraged. Another example are the debates and decisions made by economists and finance leaders about fiscal policy, which can have a significant impact on Americans financially but are often not widely understood or discussed. In addition, the administrative rules and processes that govern economic policy can also be opaque and hard to follow.

As a result, many people choose not to become invested in the fiscal policies that impact their lives, and others get lost in the breadth and complexity of the systems. This can lead to real and perceived disparities in financial health and success, which can perpetuate cycles of poverty and inequality. Whether or not these disparities are well-intentioned, it is important that the economic landscape in the United States is made more transparent, accessible, and understandable for all Americans, so that everyone can have a fair chance to achieve financial prosperity.

In the case of the Greedy Hand, the United States' tax code, regulations, financial systems, and economic processes are not always fair and equitable. Instead, they contain decisions that may benefit certain groups over others. These can take many forms, such as changes in tax laws that disproportionately benefit the wealthy, refund programs that give preferential treatment to certain industries, or the ability of the wealthy to hire expert lawyers to navigate complex legal loopholes, giving them an advantage in tax payments or wealth accumulation.

The tax code is complex and changes frequently, which can make it difficult for the average person to follow. However, the wealthy can afford to hire experts who can help them navigate the tax code and take advantage of loopholes that lower their tax bill. This can result in the wealthy paying a lower percentage of their income in taxes compared to middle- and lower-income Americans.

There are regulations and policies that benefit specific industries over others. For instance, industries that are deemed to be important for national security, politically powerful, or have a well-connected lobby, may be able to influence the government to pass regulations that benefit them while hurting others.

Furthermore, financial systems can also be designed in a way that benefits certain groups over others. For example, the wealthy may have access to financial products and services that are not available to those with lower incomes, giving them an advantage when it comes to growing their wealth.

For the Clumsy Hand, policies that are designed to promote economic opportunity and growth can sometimes have unintended consequences and result in disparities in economic outcomes. One example of this is the policy of allowing taxpayers to deduct mortgage expenses from their income taxes. This policy is well-intentioned, as it is designed to extend the financial resources of homebuyers who may otherwise be stretched to afford a home.

The policy works by allowing homebuyers to deduct the interest they pay on their mortgage from their taxable income. This makes it more affordable for them to purchase a home, as it reduces the amount of money they need to pay in taxes. As homeowners make their mortgage payments, they are also building equity in their home. This equity can be passed on to their heirs when they pass away, which can help the next generation to afford a down payment on their own home and continue the cycle of wealth accumulation in their family.

While this policy is beneficial for those who are able to take advantage of deductible mortgage interest, it can also perpetuate disparities in economic outcomes. For example, lower-income individuals may not be able to afford to purchase a home, and therefore cannot take advantage of the mortgage interest deduction. This can make it more difficult for them to accumulate wealth and pass it on to future generations.

Additionally, people who are renters may not have the same opportunity to accumulate wealth as homeowners. While that wealth growth is enhanced in some, there are many others who still had homeownership out of reach. The tax deduction does not benefit them as they strive to make their rent payments.

As people progress through their lives, they will receive some of their income from Social Security in retirement. Social Security is a government-provided retirement income program that is designed to provide a basic level of financial support for retirees. However, while Social Security provides a steady source of income for retirees, it does not provide the opportunity to accumulate household wealth.

When a person reaches the end of their life, Social Security benefits stop, and they may not have other assets, such as a family home, to pass on to future generations. This can make it difficult for the next generation to afford the expenses associated with homeownership, such as a down payment. Without the ability to accumulate wealth and pass it on to future generations, the disparities in wealth can continue to expand from one generation to the next.

A similar example holds for the rate of taxation on Capital Gains. The policy of setting the tax rate on Capital Gains at 20% is intended to encourage investment in corporations by providing a lower rate than many levels of income tax. This can have an impact on executive compensation, as executives may choose to take stock options instead of salary in order to benefit from the lower tax rate. While this can be beneficial for those who own stock and see a reduction in their tax burden, it is also viewed as unfair for those who do not own stock and must pay taxes on their ordinary income. While well intentioned to promote investment in business and industry, the policy succeeds in that effort but may ultimately lead to disparities in the distribution of wealth among different groups of individuals. The impact of a lower tax rate is certainly positive for everyone who owns stock; however it is also viewed unfairly for those who do not own stock and pay tax on their ordinary income at higher rates.

▪ The Intentional Hand

While economists have debated the role of the Invisible Hand in their economic policies and programs, no idealized version of the concept has taken hold. Adam Smith's Invisible Hand has not resulted in the benefit to the whole of society as he proposed. In its place, the hands of the clumsy and the greedy have had opportunity to influence policy which has sustained unequal benefit and access for the participants of American capitalism. What is and has always been needed is an Intentional Hand which lays the foundation for economic opportunities and success for all Americans.

The interventions that are made in America's capitalist economy should be planned and thoroughly considered for intentional outcomes. History, analysis, and reason may all play a part in new economic policy initiatives. The Intentional Hand should be used to prevent the Greedy Hand from influencing economic matters. The potential for a Clumsy Hand may be reduced using the Intentional Hand. While well meaning, unforeseen outcomes, externalities, abuse, or other exigencies may divert the intended outcomes of the Intentional Hand.

The FY100 initiative has very intentional goals.
1.   Provide everyone in the United States with a Social Security Number $100,000 in assets

2. Secure the assets until the account holder turns 65, which may then be used for any purpose

3. Supplement Social Security and other retirement income

4. Provide an asset which may be easily transferred to heirs

5. Invest the FY100 funds in a manner which promotes domestic business

6. Provide an investment return on FY100 accounts which is equal across account holders and focuses on long term success

7. Have participation in the FY100 initiative be voluntary for receivers, givers, and investment partners

8. Have the benefits of participating in the FY100 initiative be so great, that participants would be encouraged to share wealth with others and generate it for themselves

9. Limit the contributions to a person to a lifetime cap, to prevent the risk of excessive use by those who are already wealthy

10. Give participants the opportunity to benefit from the success and profits of a strong and healthy American economy

These ten goals of FY100 accounts are intentional. It is important for our leaders to highlight goals like this in any policy discussion. When the goals are intentional, and merits of the policy are debated across viewpoints and lenses that will help assure a new policy works as intended. Our economy need not be left to invisible forces.

Self-interest, Family, Friends, Community, Beyond

There is ongoing debate between different economic theories about whether individuals primarily act out of self-interest or whether there is a more cooperative nature among people can continue without hostility or animosity. This disagreement does not need to be divisive; it can be a healthy part of the ongoing conversation about how to understand and improve the economy. Each perspective brings its own insights and understanding, and ultimately, a balance of both can lead to more effective solutions for the economy. The FY100 initiative however does not need to be mired in the debate. An advantage to the FY100 initiative is that it does not matter what the motivations of the people are, as it can succeed within the lenses of competing theories where one acts in their own self interest or acts with others wellbeing in mind.

For a person or organization that acts in a more self-interested manner, the desire to reduce their own tax burden will incentivize them to participate. Since their self-interest would have them maximize the tax benefit to themself, they will do that, but only to the point of reaching their own lifetime contribution cap of $100,000 in their own account. Beyond that, to satisfy the self-interest of maximizing their tax benefit, they will need to seek out others beyond themselves to contribute to.

For those who are more cooperative and concerned about others, the FY100 initiative provides them with a novel option to help others. The tax advantage to giving helps extend the amount that they are able to give. In addition, the structure of the account enables them to give a tax-free gift which will specifically benefit the recipient in their senior years and help them build wealth.

401(k)s, 403(b)s, and 457s do not allow contributions by people other than the individual or the employer. Social Security is only earned through work and to contribute to an Individual Retirement Account the person must have earned income. With these constraints in existing programs, the FY100 account will make it easier for those who do not fit into these retirement plan criteria to accumulate wealth for their senior years. Someone who wants to give to someone else may not have been able to with these programs. This is where flexibility in receiving money is beneficial to the FY100 initiative.

Capitalism

Capitalism is an economic system that is characterized by the private ownership of the means of production, the creation of goods and services for profit, and the competition among businesses to sell those goods and services. It has its roots in the economic and political changes that occurred during the Renaissance and the Industrial Revolution.

Tracing back to the emergence of trade and commerce in ancient civilizations, it was not until the Renaissance, a period of great cultural and intellectual change in Europe, that the foundations of capitalism began to take shape. During the Renaissance, the growth of trade and commerce led to the development of a new class of merchants and entrepreneurs who were motivated by profit. These individuals were able to accumulate wealth and use it to invest in new businesses and industries. This marked the beginning of the modern concept of capital, which refers to the resources and assets that are used to produce goods and services.

The Industrial Revolution, which began in the late 18th century, also played a major role in the development of capitalism. The Industrial Revolution was a period of rapid technological and economic change, marked by the introduction of new machines and methods of production. These advances led to a significant increase in the production of goods, which in turn led to the growth of businesses and the creation of new wealth.

In the United States there is great pride in being viewed as having a capitalist economy. The FY100 initiative fits very well in many of the main principles of capitalism, including:

- Private property: Under capitalism, the means of production are privately owned, rather than being owned by the state.

  - Investors in FY100 accounts make their assets available for investment in domestic publicly traded companies. The funds for the stock purchases move from the person giving directly to the FY100 account holder, without government intervention. Since the investments are made in publicly traded companies, the funds are utilized by companies that independently made the decision to enter into that regulated market in order to access the vast amounts of capital available in that system. Privately held companies, and those in private equity markets are not compelled to participate.

- Competition: Businesses compete with each other in order to sell their goods and services at the highest price possible.

  - Not only do businesses compete for selling their goods and services, but they also compete for access to working capital. By providing a new source of stable capital, businesses may find accessing FY100 funds is beneficial to their business model.

- Profit motive: The primary goal of businesses under capitalism is to maximize profits.

  - Businesses being motivated by profit is positive for FY100 account holders. As investors in the businesses, the FY100 account holders stand to receive dividends from their common investments. When employees of a business, people will earn the wages that they have agreed to. As investors in business those same employees will share in the profit.

- Supply and demand: The price of goods and services is determined by the interplay of supply (how much is available) and demand (how much people are willing to pay).

- As consumers in an economy, people may be impacted by the variations in price, particularly when there are inflationary trends at work. Investments in business through FY100 funds will put people on both ends of the financial equation. They will be the consumers that benefit when prices are low, but also as investors will benefit when profits are higher.

- Price system: Prices are used to allocate resources and coordinate economic activity.

  - FY100 account holders will contribute directly to making funds available to business to meet their business objectives. This may be providing capital investment, funds for expanding labor, or access to commodities, raw materials, and business services. FY100 account capital enables business to have a reliable base of funds to acquire their needed resources and generate economic activity from their business.

- Laissez-faire: The government plays a minimal role in the economy, allowing individuals and businesses to operate with minimal interference.

  - Individuals and businesses decide when to transfer their funds to FY100 account holders. They are not subject to a taxation plan imposed by the government. Market conditions will dictate the dividend return on the FY100 account investments, which are free to rise and fall with the prosperity of the American economy.

- Capital accumulation: Businesses and individuals can invest their profits in order to expand and grow their businesses.

  - When a business chooses to participate in accessing capital from FY100 account holders, they know that the dividends paid back can be returned again as available capital. Businesses decide when it is in their best interest to utilize the resources and make the best decisions in their view to grow their business.

- Entrepreneurship: Capitalism encourages innovation and risk-taking through the creation of new businesses and industries.

  - One of the barriers to starting a new business is access to capital. Small businesses often start by getting investors or loans of private equity. With the expansion of investors in their FY100 accounts, there is an increasing and stable amount of new available capital coming into the economy. This new capital could bring down the cost of borrowing for entrepreneurs.

- Innovation: Capitalism promotes the development of new technologies and processes, which can lead to increased productivity and economic growth.

    - FY100 accounts have the potential to make available significant amounts of reliable capital for business use. The stability of this funding will be attractive to businesses wanting to innovate. Equity markets can be quite volatile and a business looking to invest in itself would want to have greater certainty of a stable capital investment to try out its innovations. FY100 accounts could provide the funding in a desirable time horizon to give business the confidence to undertake the innovation.

- Consumer sovereignty: Under capitalism, consumers have the freedom to choose what they want to buy, which drives the demand for goods and services.

    - Nothing about FY100 accounts inhibits consumers from exercising their sovereignty.

- Limited government intervention: The government plays a limited role in the economy, and there is a general belief in the importance of free markets and free enterprise.

    - The FY100 Initiative is specifically intended to minimize government participation. Unlike Social Security where the government collects taxes, defines benefits, and administers a program through the distribution of benefit checks, FY100 is more of a defined contribution program that is user led. Once the account is established, the account owner determines the contributions along with third party givers up to the lifetime contribution cap of $100,000. The funds are managed through the Securities and Exchange Commission to produce a dividend, however once the funds are unlocked when the account owner turns 65, the account owner decides when and how funds are used. Further, the SEC does not invest the funds directly, instead it establishes the parameters by which the publicly traded domestic businesses may choose how to access funds.

Neoliberalism

Neoliberalism is a political and economic philosophy that emphasizes free markets, limited government intervention, and individual responsibility. It has had a significant impact on the United States and other countries around the world.

The origins of neoliberalism can be traced back to the ideas of classical liberalism, which emerged in the 18th and 19th centuries and championed the concept of a free market economy. However, neoliberalism as a distinct ideology began to take shape in the 20th century, influenced by the work of economists such as Friedrich Hayek and Milton Friedman.

In the 1970s, neoliberalism gained prominence in the United States and other Western countries as a response to economic stagnation and high inflation. Neoliberals argued that the solution to these problems was to reduce government intervention in the economy and to let market forces dictate economic outcomes.

One of the key figures in the development of neoliberalism in the United States was President Ronald Reagan, who came to power in 1981. Reagan implemented a number of policies that were based on neoliberal ideas, including tax cuts, deregulation, and reduced government spending. These policies were intended to stimulate economic growth and encourage entrepreneurship.

The impact of neoliberalism in the United States has been significant. On the one hand, it has contributed to economic growth and increased international competitiveness. However, it has also been associated with income inequality and the erosion of social programs and protections for workers.

Neoliberalism has also been criticized for prioritizing the interests of corporations and wealthy individuals over those of the general public. Some have argued that this has contributed to the increasing polarization and political divide in the United States.

Neoliberalism is a political ideology and economic theory that advocates for free markets, free trade, and minimal government intervention in the economy. It is based on the belief that the free market is the most efficient and fair system for allocating resources and promoting economic growth.

Neoliberalism has been a dominant economic theory in the United States for decades. The FY100 initiative works with several aspects of neoliberal thinking, including:

- Free markets: Neoliberals believe that the free market, rather than the government, is the most efficient and fair mechanism for allocating resources and promoting economic growth.

    - Similar to the Laissez-Faire concept in Capitalism individuals and businesses decide when to transfer their funds to FY100 account holders and who they want to do that with. While there is a generous tax benefit to giving and receiving funds in an FY100 account, the businesses and individuals will decide the best means of doing that. Market conditions will dictate the dividend return on the FY100 account investments, which are free to rise and fall with the prosperity of the American economy.

- Limited government intervention: Neoliberals favor a limited role for the government in the economy and believe that the market should be allowed to function without interference.

    - A main feature of FY100 accounts is to allow people to decide how to redistribute capital in the economy. The individual lifetime contribution cap inhibits the accumulation of significant wealth in the system, however the decisions on the distribution are made without government involvement.

- Privatization: Neoliberals support the privatization of state-owned enterprises and the outsourcing of government services to the private sector.

    - This concept is not hindered by FY100 accounts. By introducing significant capital into the economy, the FY100 initiative could facilitate the ability for private businesses to undertake services traditionally performed by the government.

- Individualism: Neoliberals emphasize the importance of individual freedom and responsibility, and believe that individuals, rather than the government, should be responsible for their own well-being.

    - When it comes to providing retirement security, the FY100

initiative gives tremendous freedoms and responsibilities for individuals to care for and decide for themselves. Once a person turns 65, the funds contained within the FY100 account are all unlocked, and the account owner may use the funds however they determine best. Many people are dependent on the retirement income they get from Social Security. A successful FY100 initiative will help reduce individual reliance on Social Security income and the taxes placed on others to fund it.

- **Small government:** Neoliberals advocate for smaller government and lower taxes, as they believe that this will lead to more efficiency and economic growth.

  - In the future as more people contribute to the FY100 initiative and the assets within it are able to grow with dividends from the investments in domestic businesses, the more benefit the initiative will demonstrate. As larger portions of the population maximize the contributions to the $100,000 lifetime cap, the accounts will grow with many years of dividend income. The resources that will be necessary to provide Social Security will reduce over time. Ideally, if everyone born in the United States would receive the total contribution at the time of their birth, dividend growth over the next 65 years would provide significant funds to support the individual in their senior years. At today's birth rates, a fully funded FY100 initiative would cost less than a third of what it costs to run the Social Security program. This would mean lower taxes and less need for government to administer a Social Security program.

- **Fiscal conservatism:** Neoliberals tend to be fiscally conservative and favor balanced budgets and low levels of government debt.

  - By investing in American businesses, contributions to FY100 accounts will allow a novel system of defined contribution saving for retirement. This would allow retirement savings to grow with the American economy and reflect the demographic changes in society as birth rates either grow or contract. Shifting retirement savings to this model will lower the need for the federal government to finance future benefits.

- **Monetarism:** Neoliberals often support monetarist economic policies, which focus on controlling the money supply and inflation.

- With little action by Congress to address economic conditions within the United States, the Federal Reserve is often left to manage both the money supply and inflation through the limited tools available to it. The Federal Reserve mainly does this through adjustments to the federal funds rate in an effort to impact the cost of borrowing. By putting the FY100 initiative into place, there will be new opportunities for the Federal Reserve or others to impact the supply of money and inflation. The initiative would allow for an increase in the money supply through contributions to individual FY100 accounts. The Federal Reserve could impact inflation through the investment side of the FY100 initiative. The cost of borrowing could be raised by the Federal Reserve capturing a larger portion of the available capital for investment within the FY100 initiative. Similarly, it could lower interest rates by releasing funds to be available to the domestic public equity market businesses.

- Neoclassical economics: Neoliberals often rely on neoclassical economic theory, which emphasizes the importance of individual choice, competition, and market forces in determining economic outcomes.

- When the federal government taxes it's population and businesses, it is up to the policy decisions of Congress to decide how those resources will be utilized within the economy. By instituting the FY100 initiative, there will be more choice of the participants in the economy to decide when and how to utilize their resources. After money has been saved in an FY100 account and grows as a result of dividend accumulation, the person's account will be unlocked when they turn 65. If they decide to withdraw all of their funds at age 65 and spend them quickly, that will be their decision. Contrary to the Social Security system, where the benefits are calculated and distributed as regular payments, the funds may be spent on a schedule of the government's choosing.

Modern Monetary Theory

Modern monetary theory (MMT) is a macroeconomic theory that emphasizes the role of the government in managing the economy using fiscal and monetary policy. It suggests that governments that control their own sovereign currency, such as the United States government, have the ability to create as much money as needed to fund public goods and services, as long as they do not exceed the capacity of the economy to produce goods and services. This means that the government can fund any program or project it deems necessary by simply creating more currency, as long as it does not lead to inflation.

The roots of MMT can be traced back to the work of economists such as John Maynard Keynes, who argued that government intervention in the economy, through the use of fiscal and monetary policy, is necessary to stabilize the economy and promote full employment.

However, MMT as it is known today emerged more recently, in the 1990s, as a response to the neoclassical economic policies that were being implemented in many countries at the time, including the United States.

In the early 2000s, economists began developing and promoting MMT as a more effective alternative to neoclassical economics.

There are a number of ways that the MMT perspective can be benefitted in the American economy through the use of the FY100 initiative:

- Government spending: MMT suggests that the government can fund any program or project it deems necessary by simply creating more currency.

  - The United States has done this in recent years with stimulus payments during the Great Recession, and in response to the economic impacts of the COVID pandemic. Those funds were deployed in a variety of mechanisms including checks directly to taxpayers, stimulus payments to businesses, funding directly to local governments, and other mechanisms. While some of these options were criticized for being inflationary, using the FY100 initiative could be a means of increasing the money supply with a lower risk of inflationary pressures. If the federal government decides to contribute directly to FY100 accounts, the funds going into those would mostly become available capital for domestic firms in the public equity market. The funds that could go into the accounts of people 65 years and older would be immediately unlocked and have a more direct impact on consumer level spending. Not being able to anticipate the economic conditions under the next scenario where the federal government determines that is necessary to act, having the FY100 initiative available would be beneficial as an additional economic tool.

- Deficit spending: MMT argues that government deficit spending is not necessarily a bad thing and can actually be beneficial for the economy.

  - Like the opportunity to increase the money supply through the FY100 initiative, the federal government could direct its deficit spending into FY100 accounts. This could be a straightforward method to make funding available for domestic businesses capital needs, and benefit the individuals participating with an FY100 account at the same time. Again, this would be just another tool available to the federal government to address future economic needs.

- Inflation: MMT argues that the government can create as much currency as it wants without causing inflation, as long as it is done in a controlled manner.

  - If the federal government operates with an intentional hand, it can do so without creating new inflationary pressures. One of the features of the FY100 initiative is to reduce the volatility within the domestic public equity market. By creating a capital source that is both significant in size and available for an extended period, the FY100 initiative creates a reliable source of capital for businesses to use.

- Unemployment: MMT suggests that the government can use its ability to create currency to fund job programs and reduce unemployment.

  - While the government may create its own job programs, funding the opportunity for public businesses to grow, expand, and profit from increased labor is also desirable. The stable capital generated by the FY100 accounts can enable businesses to hire the labor that they need in addition to funding capital equipment, commodities, raw materials, or business services.

- Interest rates: MMT argues that the government can set interest rates at any level it wants, and that low interest rates can stimulate economic growth.

  - The Federal Reserve does have the ability to adjust interest rates and by lowering them, they decrease the costs of borrowing. Stimulating the economy by lowering borrowing costs is not the only means of achieving this. With the FY100 initiative, borrowing costs can be lowered by increasing the supply of capital available to business for borrowing. If the Federal Reserve has access to some of the capital available in the FY100 initiative and was paying a dividend on those assets, it could release the assets and make them available to business. The other alternative for increasing capital would be to make contributions directly into individuals FY100 accounts, thereby increasing the amount of capital available to those businesses.

- Public debt: MMT suggests that public debt is not necessarily a bad thing, and that the government can simply create more currency to pay off its debts.

  - Like the deficit spending above, if it is a desirable public policy objective to encourage more public debt, the FY100 initiative would be an effective additional tool to place the funding generated by that debt.

- Income distribution: MMT suggests that the government can use its control over the money supply and taxation to influence income distribution and reduce inequality.

  - While the FY100 initiative is envisioned to address some of the challenges of wealth inequality in society, there is a limited opportunity to address income inequality. First, when the funds within an FY100 account become unlocked when a person turns 65, they are free to use those funds however they choose. One of the ways to use those funds is to supplement income with distributions of the assets and their dividends in the account. In this regard, FY100 accounts could be an indirect way of impacting the income of people over the age of 65, especially those who do not have access to all available traditional retirement savings vehicles, like 401(k) and others.

- Economic stabilization: MMT suggests that the government can use its control over the money supply and fiscal policy to stabilize the economy and smooth out business cycles.

  - The United States economy is a tremendously complex system. When economists and policymakers desire to utilize the tools at their disposal to stabilize the economy, it would be beneficial to have an additional tool like the FY100 initiative at their disposal. It is important to repeat that one of the features of the FY100 initiative is to provide a significant and stable amount of capital that is available to domestic businesses within the public equity market. The long-term availability of these funds would itself provide for reduced volatility within the public equity market and assist in smoothing out the business cycles which today are subject to significant shocks and swings caused by public market forces.

Socialism

Socialism is a political and economic ideology that aims to create a more equal and fair society by eliminating social and economic inequalities. It advocates for the collective ownership and control of the means of production, distribution, and exchange, and for the redistribution of wealth and resources to meet the needs of all members of society. The ultimate goal of socialism is to create a more equal and just society by eliminating exploitation and inequality.

The history of socialism can be traced back to the early 19th century, with the development of theories by philosophers such as Henri de Saint-Simon and Charles Fourier. However, the modern socialist movement emerged in the late 19th and early 20th centuries, with the founding of socialist parties and the development of Marxist theory by Karl Marx and Friedrich Engels.

Marxist theory, which forms the basis of socialism, posits that capitalism, in which the means of production are owned and controlled by a small group of capitalists, is inherently exploitative and leads to the concentration of wealth and power in the hands of a few. Socialism, on the other hand, proposes the abolition of private ownership of the means of production and the creation of a classless society in which the means of production are owned and controlled by the community as a whole.

The first socialist revolutions took place in the early 20th century, with the Russian Revolution of 1917 and the Chinese Revolution of 1949. These revolutions led to the establishment of socialist governments in Russia and China, which implemented various forms of socialism, including state socialism and communist socialism.

There are many different interpretations of socialism and its principles, and different socialist movements and ideologies have emphasized different elements. However, some common principles of socialism can be advanced through the FY100 initiative:

- Collective ownership: Socialists believe that the means of production, distribution, exchange, and information should be owned and controlled collectively, rather than being owned and controlled by a small group of individuals or corporations.

     - Investments in FY100 accounts take advantage of businesses that are already participating in the public equity market. The funds that are invested expand the number of people who are investors in those publicly traded companies. Businesses that are privately held by an individual, or those that have a group of private investors or not the objects of investment by FY100 accounts. In the spirit of broader ownership, the FY100 accounts will add tens of millions more people into the ownership ranks as investors in the domestic publicly traded businesses.

- Economic democracy: Socialists believe that economic decision-making should be democratically controlled by the workers and communities who are affected by those decisions, rather than being controlled by a small group of elites or owners.

     - With the expansion of investors that comes with FY100 accounts, in order to satisfy the dividend returns sought by these new owners, the businesses will need to operate with their interests in mind. Since the resources of all of the FY100 account holders are combined for investment, there will not be a direct line of ownership from an individual with FY100 savings to any individual business. The FY shares held in each business will earn dividends, but not be voting shares. The interest of the FY100 account holders in earning a dividend from their shares will be an important consideration of the boards for these publicly traded businesses.

- Social ownership: Socialists believe that the wealth and resources of society should be owned and controlled by the whole community, rather than being owned and controlled by a small group of individuals or corporations.

     - While ownership in publicly traded businesses is available to anyone in America today, more than half of Americans do not own any stock in businesses. A specific feature of FY100 accounts is to expand the ownership of businesses in the public equity market to everyone with a Social Security number. This broad ownership will result in the profit generated by the businesses to be distributed across the population rather than remaining in the hands of a smaller number of investors.

- Redistribution of wealth: Socialists believe that wealth and resources should be redistributed more evenly, so that everyone has an equal opportunity to meet their needs and live a good life.

   - FY100 accounts are designed with the broad distribution of wealth in mind. The incentives to contribute to these accounts, the nature of the investments, and the broad access enable the business ownership through shares, and profit through dividends to be more widely available in American society.

- Economic and social equality: Socialists believe that everyone should have an equal opportunity to participate in economic and social life, and that everyone should have access to the same basic needs and rights, such as healthcare, education, and housing.

   - A key feature of FY100 accounts is the ability for anyone with a Social Security number to have an account. Compared to individual retirement accounts where someone must have earned income, FY100 accounts have a broader reach. Additionally in 401(k), 403(b), and 457 accounts require an individual to have an appointment with an employer that sponsors this type of account. The wealth that is accumulated overtime in these accounts will be available for the account holder when they turn 65. With all of the funds in the FY100 account unlocked at that time, the account holder is free to use the accumulated funds in any manner they choose including for healthcare, education, and housing.

- Social justice: Socialists believe in working towards a more just and equitable society, where everyone has an equal chance to succeed and be treated fairly, regardless of their race, gender, religion, or other characteristics.

   - There are no features of an FY100 account that prevents people from participating on the basis of race, gender, religion, or other characteristics. The only limiting factor is that the account holder must have a Social Security number. This feature makes it very broadly available to Americans.

- Decentralization: Socialists believe in decentralizing power and decision-making, so that communities and individuals have more control over their own lives and destinies.

     - While there are no features of FY100 accounts that relate to the participants having power, through participation the account holders will be accumulating wealth over time. The accumulation of wealth will help to strengthen the participants economically, and as their economic security increases, they may have more personal freedom in which to engage in civic participation.

- Cooperation: Socialists believe in the value of cooperation and mutual aid, and that we can achieve more together than we can individually.

     - A significant component of participation in FY100 is cooperation. Since there is a lifetime contribution cap on the accounts, it encourages people to help others rather than only focus on their individual wealth accumulation. A key feature of the initiative is that any individual, business, or other organization may contribute to a participating individual. This feature of cooperation is rewarded through a tax benefit for each participant; however it ultimately means that people will work together to reduce wealth inequality, and improve the fiscal security of others.

- Human rights: Socialists believe in the inherent dignity and value of every human being, and in the importance of protecting and promoting human rights for all people.

     - By broadening the access to investing in the FY100 accounts, people are not separated by their employment status, age, marital status, or other factors in participating. Everyone has the same limit on contributions, investments and the dividend returns are made in common, and everyone is free to use the funds as they best see fit when they are unlocked at the age of 65.

Libertarianism

Libertarianism is a political philosophy and movement that promotes individual liberty, free markets, and limited government. The origins of libertarian thought can be traced back to the works of classical liberals in the 18th and 19th centuries. These philosophers advocated for limited government intervention in the economy and individual freedom.

In the United States, libertarian ideas began to gain more mainstream attention in the mid-20th century, with the publication of books where Libertarian ideals were in the foreground. During the 1970s and 1980s, the libertarian movement gained momentum with the formation of organizations such as the Libertarian Party.

In recent years, libertarianism has become increasingly influential in American politics, with politicians espousing libertarian views and gaining a significant following. Libertarianism has a sizable following in the United States; however, it is a minority viewpoint in the global political spectrum. There is no single set of principles that all libertarians subscribe to, and different libertarian thinkers may emphasize different principles. The FY100 initiative shares many principles with libertarianism, including:

- Individual liberty: Libertarians believe that individuals have the right to live their lives as they see fit, as long as they respect the rights of others.

  - One of the most significant features of the FY100 initiative is that it is completely voluntary for people to establish an account, for people to contribute to others, and for businesses to use the capital accumulated in the initiative for their business enterprise. While there are tax incentives for participation, if participation in the initiative does not make sense for someone, they are not required to participate.

- Free markets: Libertarians believe in the power of free markets to allocate resources efficiently and fairly, and that government interference in the market tends to be harmful.

  - The freedom for businesses to access the available capital in the FY100 initiative is completely their choice. Businesses are free to remain individually owned, privately held among a group of investors, or they may choose to seek capital in the public equity markets. There are no features of the FY100 initiative that inhibits business from conducting itself in a manner that it best sees fit.

- Limited government: Libertarians believe that government should be limited in its scope and power, and that individuals should have as much freedom as possible to make their own decisions.

  - In an effort to reduce wealth inequality, many discuss the institution of taxes as a mechanism for the redistribution of wealth. With the FY100 initiative, participants are encouraged to take part through tax incentives, however there is no role for government in deciding who participates, how much they participate, or who they participate with.

- Voluntary exchange: Libertarians believe that people should be free to engage in voluntary exchange with one another, without interference from the government or other external parties.

  - While there is a lifetime contribution cap to funds that are put into an FY100 account, there is not a restriction on who may contribute, or to whose account a contribution can be made. Unlike existing retirement programs that have limitations on who may participate, the FY100 account is available to anyone with a Social Security number. If an individual, business, or other organization desires to contribute funds to any individuals FY100 account, they are free to do so.

- Personal responsibility: Libertarians believe that individuals should be responsible for their own actions and the consequences of those actions, and that they should not be able to shift the burden of their mistakes onto others.

  - In the context of saving for retirement, in the United States there is a significant reliance on the Social Security system. While an individual's lifetime earnings factor into the calculation for their Social Security payments, those payments are made by the working taxpayers at the time the person is drawing Social Security benefits. The FY100 initiative shifts away from a defined benefit program like Social Security, and instead encourages savings and investment in a limited contribution account. When the invested funds are unlocked when the FY100 account holder turns 65, they are free to use the accumulated funds in any manner they see fit. There are no restrictions on the use of funds and may be all spent immediately or preserved indefinitely to pass on to the account holder's heirs.

- Limited taxation: Libertarians believe that taxation should be limited, as they see it as a form of coercion and a violation of property rights.

   - A primary feature of FY100 accounts is for there to be a tax benefit to the contributor and the recipient of FY100 account contributions. The funds going into the account or not taxed, and the funds drawn from the account are not taxed either. If the accumulated balance in the account is passed on to an heir, the heir receives the funds in their FY100 account without any tax liability and may spend the inherited funds without tax liability either.

Democratic Party

The Democratic Party in the United States is one of the two major political parties in the country. The party traces its origins to the early 19th century and the Democratic-Republican Party. The Democratic Party itself was formed in 1828 by people in favor of greater democracy and individual liberty.

In the years that followed, the party generally favored a strong federal government, as well as policies such as expansion of voting rights and infrastructure development. The party's support came primarily from Northern and Western states, and it was the party of President Franklin D. Roosevelt, who served four terms in the 1930s and 1940s and led the country through the Great Depression and World War II.

During the Civil Rights Movement of the 1960s, the Democratic Party became increasingly associated with progressive social policies and civil rights for minorities. In recent years, the party has tended to support a larger welfare state and a more active government role in the economy. It also advocates for environmental protection, workers' rights, and healthcare reform.

In modern times, the Democratic Party has held the majority in the House of Representatives for most of the period since the early 1990s and has also held the presidency for the majority of the time since 1933.

The Democratic Party represents the interests of the working and middle classes and advocates for progressive policies. Principles that are often associated with the Democratic Party may also apply to the FY100 initiative:

- Social justice: The Democratic Party believes in promoting equality and fairness for all people, regardless of their background or circumstances.

    - Many policy programs seek to improve equality by providing a benefit to one group when there is a measured scarcity. A defining feature of the FY100 initiative is that it is not just available to anyone with a Social Security number, but it provides a lifetime contribution cap to the strong tax incentive of participation. Compared to a 401(k), the current annual contribution limit is now over $20,000 per year. That is a significant amount of money for the average American worker. Assuming a worker has access to a 401(k) through work, if a person contributes $20,000 per year from age 20 to age 65, they will have deposited $900,000 into that savings vehicle. Only the highest paid people would be able to do that. FY100 accounts are structured to incentive a wide distribution of contributions.

- Social welfare: The Democratic Party supports policies that provide assistance to those in need, including programs such as Social Security, Medicare, and Medicaid.

    - The social welfare programs provided by the federal government are heavily utilized, cost a significant portion of taxpayer dollars, and are under regular threat of cuts to benefits or eligible participants. For people anticipating benefits many years or decades from now, the uncertainty of the benefits being available is stressful. By offering the FY100 initiative, a strongly incentivized account is in place where defined contributions can be made, instead of an uncertain defined benefit. Broad participation in FY100 accounts will enable account holders to have a stronger sense of fiscal security for their senior years and provide a cushion for cuts to benefits that may be necessary in the future.

- Workers' rights: The Democratic Party supports policies that protect the rights of workers, including fair wages, safe working conditions, and the right to unionize.

- With the complexity in society and the variety of circumstances workers find in their personal lives, they would benefit from additional choice in their forms of compensation. By offering compensation into an FY100 account, some workers may choose to benefit in a tax advantaged manner by differing their compensation by putting some into an account that will be accessible after they turn 65. This initiative may be an important component of the wage and benefit mix available for employers to offer.

- Education: The Democratic Party supports policies that provide access to quality education for all individuals, including early childhood education and affordable higher education.

  - The cost of higher education may be a barrier for some in advancing their knowledge and future employment prospects. Families that have inherited wealth are at an advantage to have resources that can be applied toward education. Where Social Security payments are made to the individual after they pass away, unless there are survivor benefit payments, there is no inherited wealth for the next generation to use. The FY100 accounts can help families in two ways. First when an FY100 account holder accumulates assets in the account and then turns 65, they may use the assets in any manner they choose. This may even be supporting education expenses for their family member. The second way is through inherited wealth. If an FY100 account holder does not expend all their accumulated wealth after they turn 65, in the event they die, their FY100 account balance is transferred to heirs, who may use the unlocked funds in any manner they choose, including education.

- Health care: The Democratic Party supports policies that provide access to affordable and high-quality health care for all individuals, including through the expansion of public programs such as Medicare and Medicaid.

  - Similar to using FY100 savings for education, once the account holder turns 65, they may use the balance of funds in any way they choose. This may be for medical expenses that are not covered by any other means.

- Women's rights: The Democratic Party supports policies that promote gender equality and protect the rights of women, including the right to access abortion and reproductive health care.

- There are no aspects of the FY100 initiative that restricts participation on the basis of gender. The fact that every person with a Social Security number can have an account, means that women are just as able to participate as men. Consider a married couple where one is employed and the other is supported by their spouse. With Social Security, 401(k)s and similar tools for providing fiscal security later in life, the employed partner has the account in their name. If there is a divorce, the employed spouse dies, or other change, their partner may be impacted negatively with survivor benefits or a change in beneficiary on the account. If the same couple makes identical contributions into their FY100 accounts, if there is a change in circumstances, each spouse will retain full ownership of their FY100 account and its balance.

- LGBTQ rights: The Democratic Party supports policies that protect the rights of LGBTQ individuals, including the right to marry and access equal employment opportunities.

- Like the treatment of genders above, there are no limitations on FY100 accounts that cause them to be treated differently by FY100 account structure. A particular marital or relationship status is not required to fully participate in the FY100 initiative. Contributions may be made by any individual, business, or organization into any individual's account.

- Racial justice: The Democratic Party supports policies that address racial inequality and promote racial justice, including through measures such as criminal justice reform.

- Continuing the themes above with gender and identity, there are no features of FY100 accounts that inhibit participation by any race. The purpose of the FY100 initiative is to provide comprehensive access to anyone with a Social Security number. Broad access is intended to facilitate use and reduce the likelihood of disparate outcomes experienced in other systems.

Republican Party

The Republican Party in the United States is one of the two major political parties in the country. The party was founded in 1854 by a coalition of anti-slavery activists, Whigs, and Free Soilers. The party was formed as a response to the passage of the Kansas-Nebraska Act of 1854 which allowed the expansion of slavery into the territories. The name "Republican" was chosen as an allusion to the Democratic-Republican Party and the republican values of liberty and civic virtue.

In the years that followed, the party generally opposed the expansion of slavery and sought to limit the power of the federal government. The first Republican president was Abraham Lincoln, who was elected in 1860 and served from 1861-1865. Lincoln's presidency included the Civil War and the eventual abolition of slavery with the 13th Amendment.

After the Civil War, the Republican Party became associated with high tariffs and staunch support for business and industry. The party also supported voting rights for African Americans. In the 20th century, the party tended to be more conservative and favored smaller government, lower taxes, and a free market economy.

In recent years, the Republican Party has generally been associated with a more conservative ideology, including support for limited government, low taxes, and a strong national defense. The party has also tended to support traditional social values such as opposition to abortion and support for Second Amendment rights.

The Republican Party is a political party in the United States that advocates for limited government, free markets, and individual liberty. The party principles correspond well with several aspects of the FY100 initiative:

- Limited government: The Republican Party believes in a small and limited government that is responsible for providing only essential services.

   - The FY100 initiative is structured to minimize the role of the government in the free transfer of wealth between individuals. The very favorable tax benefits remove government from the transfer of assets between people, and actually encourages it from a tax perspective compared to alternatives. When the FY100 account holder turns 65, they are free to spend their funds, or not spend them as they see fit. Compare this to Social Security, 401(k), 403(b), and 457 accounts which all require minimum distribution amounts. Funds in a Health Savings Account are tax advantaged, however only if spent on qualifying health expenses. A person with no significant health challenges would not be able to redeploy those funds without a fiscal consequence. Further, as a defined contribution type program, with a lifetime contribution cap, there is no need for the government to administer the distribution or use of funds once the account holder turns 65 and the money in the account is unlocked. For Social Security, the government must continue to stay involved to ensure the defined benefit of funds is appropriately distributed.

- Individual freedom: The Republican Party supports policies that protect individual freedom and autonomy, including the right to privacy and the freedom to make personal choices.

   - At the time the funds in an individual's FY100 account are unlocked, the account holder may use the funds in any manner they see fit. If a person does not wish to establish an account, they do not have to. If a person chooses not to contribute to their account or to anyone else's FY100 account, they have the individual freedom not to do so. While the tax advantages are intended to be very favorable, unlike a tax, the individual is not required to participate.

- Free markets: The Republican Party believes in the power of free markets to drive economic growth and prosperity, and supports policies that minimize government interference in the economy.

   - Businesses that participate in the public equity markets made a decision to be subjected to that regulated environment in exchange for the ability to access the significant amount of capital available for their business use. Businesses may be independently owned or have a group of private investors. Those that choose this route will raise capital through their own investors or pursue one of many conventional financing options. For those businesses that do access public equity markets, they may utilize the existing stock investment systems, or they could seek capital funding from FY100 accounts. The nature of FY100 funds is that the specialized FY shares are each worth $1 and only generate a return by the business paying back a dividend for each share, which is reinvested back into FY100 accounts. Businesses are free to decide if this means of raising capital is best for them, or if they prefer to utilize other resources.

- Fiscal conservatism: The Republican Party advocates for responsible fiscal policies, including balanced budgets and low taxes.

   - The greater the participation with FY100 accounts, the greater potential there is for the federal government to expand its fiscal conservatism. The FY100 accounts are designed for wealth to be accumulated and then be available after the account holder turns 65. With the funds being available to provide additional fiscal security for a person's senior years, a successful FY100 initiative will be able to reduce the stress in the Social Security system. Healthy balances in FY100 accounts, which have grown over time, will enable the federal government to relieve the pressure felt by the structure of the system for Social Security. Instead of a defined benefit that is paid to seniors by the current workforce, each individual is invested in themselves. This reduces the burden caused by large demographic shifts in population which may strain the ability to pay benefits in real time. A strong defined contribution program, if ideally invested at the time of birth, could cost a third of what the current Social Security system costs.

- Limited regulation: The Republican Party supports policies that minimize regulation, particularly in the business sector.

   - The benefit for an individual who has invested funds into an FY100 account also creates benefits in the business sector. The funds that become available through millions of new investment accounts will be available to the businesses in the public equity markets. The funds that are available may have time horizons of years or even decades where they are locked and available for use in business capital investments. These funds will be very attractive to business due to their predictability and stability. Businesses that are looking for funds to invest in capital, raw materials, commodities, or business services should see the very low volatility in this equity source as very attractive. As a result, accessing these funds and providing a dividend in return for their use will be beneficial to businesses.

- Pro-business: The Republican Party often supports policies that are favorable to businesses, including low taxes and limited regulation.

- The FY100 initiative is very positive for individuals in that it provides a highly tax advantaged means of investing and building wealth. It will create millions of investors whose money is used as a capital source for business. This will be very attractive for businesses that seek capital through the public equity markets. Millions of new investors bringing billions of new capital is always positive for business, however this funding will be additionally beneficial due to its stability. Assuming an even spread of age distribution of FY100 account holders, the typical funds available will be locked for 30 years or more. The Securities and Exchange Commission will certainly offer opportunities to utilize this capital on shorter time frames, however even those will be viewed as more reliable than the equity investments that businesses are used to receiving in the public equity markets.

8

FY100 - HOW ABOUT A WEALTH TAX?

To combat the inequality among Americans there are many ideas for reducing wealth inequality. One of the most common ideas proposed is for a wealth tax to be implemented on the rich, and in some manner redistribute the funds to others. Below are five substantial challenges to be resolved for a wealth tax to work.

Wealth Can Move

If a person does not like the neighborhood they are living in, they can either sell their home or not renew their lease. After choosing a neighborhood they like better, they will purchase a new home or enter into a new lease. For those with limited financial resources, this can be more challenging. The amount to purchase the home in the new community may be more than what the current home could be sold for. The cost for moving, financing a loan, and related costs could make that decision to relocate difficult or impossible.

For a wealthy individual, they don't have the same barriers to relocating their home. If the home they are selling takes a loss and they must spend more on the new home, the wealthy person just needs to decide if they want to do it. They have the money to make the move, so barriers of price do not impact them as much. Likewise, if the cost of living in their community becomes too high. A wealthy person finds it easier to overcome the barriers of relocating than other people.

In other categories, like where to locate a business, where to invest in property, and where they spend their time, all gets easier and easier to change with the greater wealth of the person. This is certainly the case with money, stocks, personal property, and other forms of wealth that can be moved more easily for a wealthy person.

Wealthy individuals may already be making decisions on where to live, invest, and operate their businesses based upon the tax environment or other fiscal factors. By making a change to the fiscal environment that the wealthy person is operating in, they may decide to evaluate other locations which are more favorable to them financially.

Wealthy people get professional tax advice from an experienced attorney or accountant and stay up to date on changes in tax laws and regulations in their current location. When they seek to move their wealth; they can make decisions on where it is best for them to be. The costs to them to move their wealth can be less than staying in place and bearing the costs of the new wealth tax or other fiscal regulation.

There are many existing systems in place that provide for the relocation of assets and people. A wealthy business owner may:

- Set up a trust in a jurisdiction with favorable tax laws.
- Establish a holding company in a tax-friendly jurisdiction.
- Invest in real estate or other assets in a country with lower tax rates.
- Use tax-efficient investment vehicles, such as exchange-traded funds or index funds.
- Seek out tax treaty benefits by investing in a country with which the individual's current country has a tax treaty.
- Utilize offshore banking or financial services in a country with lower tax rates.
- Establish a foreign pension plan or retirement account in a country with lower tax rates.
- Transfer ownership of assets to a spouse or domestic partner who resides in a country with lower tax rates.
- Donate assets to a charitable organization or foundation in a country with lower tax rates.
- Establish a foreign business and relocate income-generating activities to the new country.
- Seek out residence-based taxation in a country with lower tax rates, rather than citizenship-based taxation.
- Utilize tax-deferred exchange programs to sell and purchase assets in a tax-efficient manner.
- Seek professional tax advice from an experienced attorney or

accountant.
•   Keep up to date on changes in tax laws and regulations in both the individual's current country and the country where they are seeking to move their wealth.

Individuals may use wealth transfer strategies to manage their assets in a legal and responsible manner, just as businesses do. Some strategies that are used include:

•   Draft a will or trust to specify how wealth should be distributed after the individual's death.
•   Set up a charitable foundation or make charitable donations.
•   Transfer assets to a family member or other individual through a gift.
•   Establish a family limited partnership or limited liability company to hold and manage assets.
•   Purchase life insurance to provide financial security for loved ones.
•   Use tax-advantaged investment vehicles, such as 401(k) plans or individual retirement accounts (IRAs), to save for retirement.
•   Engage in estate planning to minimize taxes on inherited wealth.
•   Use tax-deferred exchange programs to sell real estate or other assets without triggering a tax liability.
•   Invest in assets that are taxed at a lower rate, such as municipal bonds or certain types of real estate.
•   Set up a retirement plan for a small business or self-employment.
•   Invest in annuities to provide a steady stream of income in retirement.
•   Participate in a pension plan or other employer-sponsored retirement benefit program.
•   Seek the advice of a financial planner or tax professional to identify strategies for managing wealth in a responsible and tax-efficient manner.
•   Review and understanding the tax laws and regulations that apply to a specific situation and take steps to comply with those laws.

These and other strategies are already employed by businesses and individuals seeking to minimize tax exposure or gain other financial advantages. A further tax on wealth would provide additional incentive for people to seek options to avoid the wealth tax.

The federal government turns taxes into services and income, not wealth

Assuming the government is able to capture additional taxes through a wealth tax program is a first step to reducing wealth inequality. The next challenge would be for the government to distribute those collected funds in a manner that would effectively reduce wealth inequality. The United States federal government does not have programs in place to reduce wealth inequality. At best, the majority of federal government spending provides some aid to current spending, which in theory could afford some the opportunity to invest in wealth building assets. Historically, this has not been the case and evidence showing that new wealth taxes would lead to a proportional reduction in wealth inequality does not exist. Common uses of federal revenue fund a wide range of programs and activities, including:

• National defense: This category includes military spending, as well as homeland security and international affairs. It accounted for about 15% of federal spending in 2020. – With significant spending on labor, commodities, services, and varied assets, defense spending is a reliable source of federal spending that broadly impacts the national economy.

• Social security: This program provides retirement and disability benefits to qualifying individuals. It was the largest category of federal spending in 2020, accounting for about 24% of the budget. – These funds are a source of retirement income and while the dollars are quickly spent in the economy, they are mostly consumptive purchases and do not lead to substantive reductions in wealth inequality.

• Medicare: This program provides health insurance for seniors and some disabled individuals. It accounted for about 13% of federal spending in 2020. – The spending is completely consumptive. The recipients of this funding receive medical services in exchange for the spending. Increases in spending here do benefit public health, but the opportunities for wealth accumulation with this spending rests with the providers of the medical services.

• Health: This category includes funding for various health programs, such as Medicaid and the Children's Health Insurance Program (CHIP). It accounted for about 9% of federal spending in 2020. – Like Medicare spending, this category accrues health and service benefits to the recipients. Any opportunity for wealth accumulation would most likely go to the service providers.

• Income security: This category includes programs that provide financial assistance to low-income individuals and families, such as Temporary Assistance for Needy Families (TANF) and the Supplemental Nutrition Assistance Program (SNAP). It accounted for about 10% of federal spending in 2020. – This funding would most similarly relate to Social Security spending, but instead for fiscally distressed people. Additionally, these funds are more targeted in their application and would be nearly all consumptive and likely used near immediately. There is virtually no opportunity for wealth growth associated with this category of federal spending.

- Education and training: This category includes funding for K-12 education, higher education, and job training programs. It accounted for about 3% of federal spending in 2020. – This federal spending would have a very indirect opportunity to impact wealth inequality. Recipients of these services would be able to secure better employment prospects in the future, which may lead to new wealth building capacity. This would depend of the effectiveness of the education and training offered. Since this spending has a long history in the United States, the existing wealth inequality would show that continued spending here, likely would not address this issue.

- Transportation: This category includes funding for infrastructure projects, such as roads, bridges, and public transportation. It accounted for about 3% of federal spending in 2020. – This category of spending would be similar to the national defense category. The spending is a good vehicle for a broad economic benefit, but not one that directly relates to wealth inequality.

- Veterans' benefits and services: This category includes funding for programs that provide financial and medical assistance to veterans and their families. It accounted for about 6% of federal spending in 2020. – Related to a few other categories of federal spending, but targeted toward veterans, this spending does not have programs that relate directly to building wealth among the veteran community.

- Administration of justice: This category includes funding for law enforcement, the courts, and other justice-related activities. It accounted for about 2% of federal spending in 2020. – Applied across the nation, the funding in this category provides employment opportunities associated with the delivery of these services and general economic benefit to the economy as a whole. This service has no component that addresses wealth inequality.

- General government: This category includes funding for various activities related to the operation of the federal government, such as the legislative and executive branches. It accounted for about 2% of federal spending in 2020. – Similar to the other categories that provide a general benefit to the American economy, the spending is overall positive. The challenge remains, as with the other major categories of federal spending, there are not any effective programs in place that are reducing wealth inequality.

The reality that must be faced is that no new tax, even if it is able to be collected will be able to address wealth inequality in the United States today. The program of spending by the federal government has been very similar for decades, and in that time wealth inequality has only grown. A novel system needs to be put into place that will directly address wealth inequality. More spending in existing federal spending patterns will not address it.

Trust in Government is Low

Trust in government refers to the level of confidence and belief that people have in their government's ability to make decisions and policies that are in the best interest of the public. It involves having faith in the government's competence, integrity, and commitment to serving its citizens. It is difficult to quantify the current level of trust in government in the United States, as it can vary depending on the specific measures used and the specific period being considered. However, it is generally accepted that trust in government in the United States has declined in recent decades.

Trust in the federal government has fluctuated over the past few decades, with periods of relatively high trust in the late 1960s and early 1970s with around 70% of Americans saying they trusted the federal government to do what is right. Trust in government declined significantly in the late 1970s and early 1980s, and by the 2010s, that number had dropped to around 20% of Americans saying they trust the federal government to do what is right.

Trust in government can vary significantly between different levels of government in the United States. Trust in the federal government is generally lower compared to trust in state and local governments.

State and local governments have a direct and visible presence in the daily lives of citizens, often being direct service providers, which can lead to higher levels of trust. Federal government policies and actions, on the other hand, often have a wider impact on society and can be more controversial, which may lead to lower levels of trust. Other reasons for lack of trust in the federal government include:

- Political polarization and gridlock: As the political divide has grown in recent years, it has become increasingly difficult for the federal government to pass legislation and make decisions, leading to a feeling among some that the government is not effectively addressing important issues.

• Lack of transparency and accountability: Many people believe that the federal government is not transparent enough in its actions and does not hold elected officials accountable for their decisions.

• Corruption and special interests: The perception that federal government officials are influenced by special interest groups or are involved in corruption leads to a lack of trust in government.

• Inadequate response to crises: The federal government's response to crises such as natural disasters may be perceived as slow or inadequate, leading to mistrust.

• Perceived lack of representation: Some people may feel that their interests and needs are not being represented by the government, leading to a lack of trust in government.

• Inadequate social services: People may lose trust in government when they perceive that social services such as healthcare, education and welfare are not provided adequately.

• Economic inequality: High levels of economic inequality can lead to a lack of trust in government, as people may feel that the government is not working to address issues of poverty and economic inequality.

With the lack of trust for the federal government having grown over decades one of the outcomes is that people will not have confidence in how new taxes would be utilized. If there were higher levels of trust and the federal government would deliver on its promises to provide the benefits Americans expect, there might be more support for a wealth tax. Absent the trust and the follow through, an initiative like FY100 for reducing wealth inequality would have more appeal because the government would empower and encourage people to act on their own behalf and in the best interests of others to reduce wealth inequality.

▪ Using FY100 to Rebuild Federal Government Trust

There is an opportunity for the Federal Government to utilize the Fund Your Hundred initiative to help restore and build trust. The establishment and ongoing operation of the FY100 initiative requires action by the Federal Government. There are several steps through FY100 implementation that relate directly to increased trust. These include:

• Increase transparency: The Federal Government should be transparent about its decision-making processes and make information about its activities easily accessible to the public. During the discussion of FY100 implementation by elected officials and administrators there is opportunity for those conversations to happen in a public facing manner. When the public has opportunity to see the development of the initiative, it will reduce the potential of misinformation that comes with an opaque process. Legislators can have their discussions on the merits of the initiative in the open during public hearings. This would enable their constituents to see their positions and arguments, rather than debate happening behind closed doors.

• Strengthen ethics regulations: The government should establish and enforce strong ethical standards for public officials and implement measures to prevent conflicts of interest. Since the proposed method of investing FY100 funds involves the establishment of criteria by the Securities and Exchange Commission, the initiative offers an opportunity to be ethically advantageous. When government officials choose companies in the course of carrying out public business, there can be questions about why an individual company was selected as a contractor, vendor, or recipient of an economic incentive or bailout. When the securities and exchange commission establish the criteria for receiving FY100 funds, the government would not be deciding which business receives those funds directly. Instead, the publicly traded businesses would apply to receive the funds made available by the SEC and would receive the funds as long as they met the pre-established criteria. This process inverts the means of investing funds, by having the business select the investment return it will promise, instead of government officials picking a business.

• Reduce corruption: The government should take measures to prevent corruption, such as establishing strong whistleblower protections, increasing penalties for corrupt behavior, and improving oversight mechanisms. The system described in the section above about strengthening ethics regulations, also applies to the way that the FY 100 initiative can reduce corruption. When the investment criteria are clearly laid out in advance for the businesses to choose from, the public and others have the opportunity to see the investment parameters. Businesses would only be able to choose from those. This process can help to reduce the chance of corrupt actors.

• Address inequalities: The government should work to reduce inequalities in society, including economic and social inequalities. A foundational aspect of the FY100 initiative is to address inequality. By the federal government putting this initiative into place, it will show that it cares about having a means of reducing wealth inequality. The FY 100 initiative has the greatest potential to reduce any quality than any other federal program currently in existence.

• Improve public services: The government should prioritize improving the quality and accessibility of public services, such as healthcare, education, and transportation. While the FY100 initiative would not directly improve public services, it would increase the resources for individuals to be able to access them. In the United States there is A significant amount of expense for healthcare, education, and transportation which is borne directly by the individual. By increasing the wealth resources that individuals have, they will be in a better position to access these public services which are not fully supported by the federal government today.

• Improve communication: The government should work to improve its communication with the public, including providing clear and accurate information about its policies and activities. The very nature of the FY100 initiative would require a great deal of open and clear communication with the public. Since every individual with a Social Security number would be eligible to participate in the initiative, it is essential that the initiative requirements be clear, fully explained, and readily accessible for all participants. A successful effort in communicating the FY100 initiative would benefit the federal government in demonstrating its ability to provide information to its constituents.

• Increase public participation: The government should engage with the public in meaningful ways, such as soliciting feedback, input on policy decisions and equal access to programs. Many federal programs are only available to a portion of the population, and others which are available to everyone are only able to be accessed during a portion of the person's life. Fewer programs and investments are available to everyone throughout their lives. The FY100 initiative would be available to everyone with a Social Security number. This means that people will be less likely to be critical of the initiative, compared to a program available to only a select group.

• Enhance cybersecurity: The government should prioritize cybersecurity measures to protect sensitive information and prevent cyber-attacks. The FY100 initiative would provide a new opportunity for the federal government to launch a novel initiative that is interfaced readily through computer systems. A successful effort to build in security and reliability will be a means to enhance the government's credibility and trust in this area.

• Increase civic education: The government should invest in civic education programs to help people understand how the government works and how they can participate in the democratic process. As a very broadly utilized initiative, the federal government will need to communicate how the FY100 initiative works, how it can be accessed, and the purpose and benefits of the initiative. This provides a new opportunity to connect with the public to discuss the government's role in service delivery, economics, retirement, business, and more.

• Improve responsiveness: The government should be responsive to the needs and concerns of the public and take action to address them in a timely manner. By establishing this novel initiative, the government has the opportunity to build the FY100 initiative as one that is efficient and responsive to its constituency. Not being burdened by legacy bureaucracy, the initiative can be established to be nimble and respond effectively to participant needs.

• Encourage innovation: The government should encourage innovation in its policies and programs and support the development of new technologies and approaches. Just the fact that the FY100 initiative would be established, would demonstrate a significant innovation for the public. While the initiative itself is very innovative, the funds that accrue for investment would be available to encourage innovation within the publicly traded domestic businesses. Investing in American businesses is a well-accepted value. Providing a new source of funding to continue their strong legacy of innovation would be viewed very positively.

The government should take these steps to build trust with the public. These areas, supported through the implementation of the FY100 initiative, would demonstrate its commitment to transparency, ethics, accountability, and more. The low levels of public trust in the federal government today are a reason why a wealth tax and other initiatives would be ineffective, or face resistance. The FY100 initiative is uniquely positioned to serve as a means of rebuilding public trust across a wide slate of factors.

As Americans spend their income, it increases the wealth of the wealthy

I have not explored the additional administrative burden on the Internal Revenue Service that would be necessary to implement a wealth tax, however, let's assume that is addressed and a wealth tax is put into place. The federal government collects the tax, and instead of spending on current federal programs it is distributed evenly among all citizens. It will be a small amount, just a few hundred dollars a year to each person, but nonetheless, new income to Americans.

The distribution of this new money will not fundamentally change the underlying structure of the economy which is necessary for a lasting impact on wealth inequality. It will just exacerbate the trend that currently exists with a widening wealth gap.

America most recently saw this with the federal stimulus and direct payments made to taxpayers related to the effects of the pandemic. In this scenario, there was a significant increase in commodity spending. Outside of a pandemic, the spending patterns may have shown not such a large change in commodity spending, with some spending going to additional services in the economy. There was an increase in savings, however most Americans did not save more, they spent what came in. Following the spending came an inflationary impact on the economy. Economists will study and debate the level of the stimulus and whether that contributed to inflation, or if pandemic impacts on international supply, geopolitical challenges impacting the cost of energy, or other factors were what was most responsible.

The unmistakable direct result of the additional spending was an increase to the wealth of the richest Americans, and those who had ownership stakes in the biggest businesses. This was reported and most often based upon the increasing stock value of publicly traded companies.

Debate can be had about the individual circumstances; however the underlying structure of the economy remains the same. Those that own the channels of distribution, the means of production, the systems of exchange, and the archives of information will profit when Americans spend money.

If billionaires are taxed more on their wealth, and that money is redistributed, people will spend it, mostly on immediate commodities and services that they need. When that money is spent in the existing economy, those who profited before will profit again. Nothing will have changed regarding the growth of wealth inequality. The flow of money will pay workers, who pay taxes, buy goods and services, provide revenue to businesses who spend on labor, commodities, business services, raw materials and more. But also, what will not have changed is that the owners of distribution, production, exchange, and information will profit from their place within that flow of money. A tax will just mean that the money will need to flow through a little more before it returns to the owners of distribution, production, exchange, and information.

There is not enough wealth held by the wealthy to make a meaningful change to those with no wealth

As discussed earlier in the book, there is not enough wealth held by wealthy Americans to make a meaningful difference to the lives of most Americans if it is all redistributed. Combined, America's billionaires have less than 5 trillion dollars. Five trillion is an incredibly large number.

5,000,000,000,000. Another large number is the population of the United States at over 330 million people. 330,000,000. Equally divided, that is $15,151 per person.

$15,000 is not a small amount of money to many people. Today, that would not cover most rent for a year. It will not buy most cars. It would buy one year of tuition at some schools. It would be a 20% down payment on a $75,000 house. It would also exhaust all the wealth of all the billionaires.

A new structure is needed in the economy to build the wealth of every American. A 2% wealth tax on billionaires, that generates about $100 billion annually only gets about $300 per American per year in new revenue.

In order to generate a meaningful impact to wealth accumulation, every American needs to begin accumulating wealth in the same means as the wealthy do. Ownership in the means of production. Ownership in the channels of distribution. Ownership in the systems of exchange. Ownership in the archives of information. As those publicly traded systems grow, so does the wealth of their new owners. The money brought into FY100 accounts would be reinvested back into the businesses to strengthen them and the economy as a whole. As the economy grows, more people will have an ownership stake in the means of production, distribution, exchange, and information. The gap in wealth inequality will be able to begin to shrink, between everyone, as ownership is more widely held.

9
FY100 - CONCLUSION

When we consider the various challenges facing society, they are incredibly complex and multifaceted. These challenges can take many forms, such as economic struggles, social issues, environmental concerns, or conflicts related to personal beliefs. One of the most challenging aspects of these issues is that they are often interconnected and interdependent. For example, a solution that addresses an economic challenge may have unintended negative consequences for the environment, or a strategy that aims to improve social conditions may end up exacerbating economic inequality. This interconnectedness makes it difficult to find effective solutions and creates a need for a holistic approach that takes into account the many different dimensions of these challenges.

I have approached the idea for Fund Your Hundred to begin to address wealth inequality. The economic challenges in American society were not created quickly, and they reach deeply into many other aspects of society. The focus here on wealth inequality is in no way intended to minimize the importance of other issues, in particular income inequality, which is often viewed as inextricably linked to wealth. For the many ways that FY100 does not address other important issues is well understood. As stated in the book, this initiative does 'not bake bread'.

The structure of FY100 was devised with the specific goal of directly addressing wealth inequality, and not being yet another program that provides an opportunity to build wealth, but is only accessible to the wealthy, ultimately creating more inequality. A key example to this is the 401(k) plan, which has been a tremendous resource for people to save for retirement. It is heavily used, and many businesses shifted away from traditional pension plans to the defined contribution model of 401(k)s. Its structure, while very popular, is not available to people who do not work, not available to millions more whose employer do not provide access, and with individual contributions enables wealthier participants the ability to use the tax advantages significantly more than someone who is lower paid.

In order to be an attractive wealth building initiative, the tax benefits on both contributions and withdrawals needed to be very strong in the FY100 initiative. They are in place with the intent of being a tremendously attractive place to put money. In order to prevent overuse by the wealthy, the individual lifetime contribution cap of $100,000 was developed. This novel idea of a lifetime cap instead of an annual contribution cap helps to ensure it is not overused by a few.

The combination of the lifetime cap and the very strong tax benefits for contributors is intentional. This creates an incentive for employers and others to look for new people to contribute to. This is the main method of reducing wealth inequality, encouraging those with assets to give more to those who don't.

To maximize participation, every person with a Social Security number is eligible. Employment status, age, income, and other factors are not relevant and enable every American to participate. The other broad participation aspect is to allow any person, business, organization, or government to give to the account holder. It is not limited to close family giving gifts, or employers making contributions, there are no limits to the relationship between who gives and who receives. Since the giver has no limit, a business can give to an employee's child, a customer, or a business colleague. This facilitates the distribution of wealth and is only bound by how much tax advantage the giver would like to utilize. No person is required to give, nor is anyone required to receive funds in their FY100 account. The initiative is very positive in that it is incentive driven, and not motivated by consequences.

When looking at a defined contribution program, one of the challenges is that investment performance can vary greatly among participants depending on the investments chosen as well as market conditions. The FY100 initiative is designed to be a wealth distribution vehicle. This resulted in the idea that any investment returns would be pooled, and all participants would receive the same return on their contributions. The millionaire with $100,000 in an FY100 account would not earn any more dividend than a laborer with $100,000 in their account.

The further challenge with wealth redistribution is the need to limit the chance of principal loss in the investments. This leads to the investment structure of these funds to be dividend producing only. The participants' shares would have a constant base value of $1.00 each, but the return would come from reinvested dividends. By being available to publicly traded domestic firms, the businesses choosing to utilize the FY100 assets in their business would already be regulated and would be encouraged to make financial decisions that advantage their investors over the long term.

What may be viewed as a liability to the FY100 initiative is the funds being locked until the account holder turns 65. This is purposeful for the intent of this being a wealth building program. Allowing withdrawals sooner or having penalty provisions for early withdrawals defeats the purpose of building $100,000 in wealth. The strict provision ensures the growth of the funds over time, and that it is not just a means of getting new tax free income. The government is forgoing tax revenue, and in exchange for that, long term investment in the American economy is the reward. That reward will be shared by everyone.

When it comes time for withdrawal when the funds are unlocked, there is again complete freedom for the account holder with how they choose to use their money. If they found it hard to accumulate assets during their working years, the FY100 account will have modest wealth they would not have otherwise had access to. For those who do not need the assets for themselves, they may be used for others, or bequeathed to another for their use, and the building of family and generational wealth.

The FY100 initiative is designed to be an Intentional Hand that encourages saving, encourages wealth distribution, and provides a mechanism for its success. Americans have been living in a society with an Invisible Hand at play in the economy. At times it is Greedy, and other times the hand is Clumsy. Whatever way you view the Invisible Hand, it has led to an American society with increasing wealth inequality. Let us use the Intentional Hand and put the Fund Your Hundred initiative into place and encourage everyone to participate, for themselves and for others.

ABOUT THE WRITER

The writer of FY100 - Fund Your $100,000 A Novel Initiative to Reduce Wealth Inequality is Daniel Mears. This is Daniel's first book and captures just some of his ideas about how to address wealth inequality in the United States. Professionally, Daniel has worked managing local governments for over 25 years. He has managed four local governments in two states.

Daniel's education culminated with a Master's degree in Public Policy Administration from the University of Missouri - St. Louis, where he developed his skills thinking about and analyzing government policy issues.

Throughout his career working in local government, he has been dedicated to addressing issues that have a direct impact on the residents he serves. With a focus on problem-solving, it is crucial for him to find solutions that not only effectively address the issue at hand, but also benefit the community and do not create additional problems. His immersion in this field has allowed him to gain a deep understanding of the unique challenges and needs of his community on behalf of his constituents and colleagues.

Daniel has worked with all levels of government over his career and has the opportunity to see close up the impacts of state and federal policies.

Maureen, Daniel's wife, is a political scientist by training, with her Masters also from UM-St. Louis. His adult son, Danny, is a full-time college student, who has already begun work in public service and has a strong interest in public policy.

9 7 9 8 2 1 8 2 3 1 3 4 7